LONDON

A Guide for
Curious Wanderers

LONDON

A Guide for
Curious Wanderers

Jack Chesher

Illustrations by Katharine Fraser

FRANCES
LINCOLN

Contents

Introduction

I firmly believe London is the world's greatest playground for the curious wanderer. Walking its streets is a fascinating journey through history with a surprise, unusual tale or hidden historical detail around every corner.

Over its nearly 2,000 years of existence, from the Romans to today, London has been shaped, moulded and changed by a variety of shifting powers and influences, with each era leaving behind its ephemera of historical remnants, details and symbols. These little relics, cut adrift from their historical context, are now anchored stubbornly in the modern metropolis and can be used to uncover its secrets.

"LONDON IS A WORLD BY ITSELF."

THOMAS BROWN

London's extraordinary variety makes it the most endlessly fascinating, enthralling and addictive city in the world to simply wander around.

In this guide to the metropolis for curious wanderers I will take you through all of my favourite details and oddities around London, each one a fascinating window into the city's past. The aim is to give you the ability to 'read' London, as well as to show you lots of new hidden corners to explore. The beautiful illustrations accompanying many of the entries should also be a useful aid in your explorations.

The book is split into the following four key chapters:

Stepping Through Time is a romp through the ages, looking at the clues you can find on London's buildings, from Roman ruins to the glittering skyscrapers of today. What can you tell about a building from the size of its window and where can you find London's least secretive secret bunker?

Cracking the Capital's Code focuses on the plethora of symbols and names you can find around the city and how to decipher them. Where did the name Bleeding Heart Yard come from, why is

"TO WALK ALONE IN LONDON IS THE GREATEST REST."

VIRGINIA WOOLF

the symbol of St Giles a wounded deer and why can you see pineapple symbols all over London?

Part of the Street Furniture looks at the functional items that Londoners and tourists alike walk past without paying them any notice. I aim to show that the ordinary can in fact be extraordinary, from a bollard that was once a French cannon to a bench in the shape of a camel and a World War Two stretcher repurposed as a fence.

Lastly, in It's Only Natural, we are going back to basics. Travelling through the millennia, this chapter covers the elemental forces that have shaped the area we know as London, from the 'lost' rivers right through to the green spaces of the modern urban landscape, such as the tiny pocket parks hidden inside the City of London.

Each chapter also ends with a map for a themed self-guided walk, taking you on a winding route through the city's streets to see lots of the spots highlighted in the book. Feel free, however, to go off-piste should you want to.

So pop on a sturdy pair of shoes and remember, fortune favours the bold!

I. STEPPING THROUGH TIME

London is a famously unplanned city. Walk its streets and you will see a whole variety of architectural styles, arranged around, what is in many cases, a medieval street pattern. It is this that almost ensures that there is a surprise around every corner in London. Join me as we gallop through 2,000 years of London's history, looking at some of the key architectural styles through the ages and a selection of the best little details that can give us clues to that building's past.

Laying Foundations
(AD 47–1066)

FROM THE ROMANS TO THE ANGLO-SACS

Paving the Way

What: *Roman flooring*
Where: *All Hallows by the Tower, EC3R 5BJ;*
St Bride's Church, EC4Y 8AU

The Romans founded London, or Londinium, in around AD 47 and the city remained under Roman rule until around AD 410. In modern times, due to the ground level rising over the centuries with each generation's detritus and debris, sections of Roman flooring or pavement are often uncovered far below the surface in church crypts. You can see a section of tessellated flooring from a domestic dwelling in the crypt of All Hallows by the Tower and a section of Roman pavement in the crypt of St Bride's Church.

Gladiators and Executions

What: *London's Roman Amphitheatre*
Where: *Guildhall Yard, EC2V 5AE*

To see the site of a remarkable archaeological discovery, head to the heart of the City of London.

In 1988 a Roman amphitheatre was discovered 8 metres (26 feet) below the yard of the Guildhall. The amphitheatre would have hosted animal blood sports, gladiatorial contests, executions and other public spectacles. First built from wood in around AD 70, it was replaced with a more substantial stone structure in the 2nd century.

You can visit the ruins for free inside Guildhall Art Gallery, but look to the floor outside the front entrance and you will see the extent of the 80-metre (260-feet)-wide outer wall marked by a giant circle of black paving stones.

Roman Relics

What: Remains of the Roman Wall
Where: London Wall Car Park, EC2V 5DY;
Cooper's Row, EC3N 2LY

The most tangible reminders of the Roman period in London's history are the remains of the Roman wall.

The wall was constructed in around AD 200 and defined the shape of the city right up until the 17th century. It was built primarily from Kentish ragstone and was one of the largest construction projects in Roman Britain. It was then enhanced with extra towers and defences throughout the medieval period.

The remaining sections of wall today look almost cut adrift in the modern city, surrounded by glass and steel. You will find sections of wall in some unusual places. One particularly surprising location is in bay 53 of the underground London Wall car park. There is also a particularly well-preserved section just off Cooper's Row, which has an opening through which you can actually walk.

You can identify the Roman sections of the wall by the rows of terracotta tiles running horizontally along them. This was a technique used by the Romans to maintain an even height during construction and to aid stability. These can be seen clearly on the section by Tower Hill station.

The Arch of History

What: An Anglo-Saxon arch
Where: All Hallows by the Tower, EC3R 5BJ

The Romans left Britain in the 5th
century, and over the following centuries,
migratory groups, such as the Angles
and Saxons, settled in Britain. The
Anglo-Saxon period, which lasted until
1066, unfortunately, has little to show for
itself today, with most buildings being
constructed from degradable timber
and thatch.

All Hallows by the Tower
claims to be the oldest church in
the City of London, established
by Erkenwald, Bishop of
London, in AD 675. Most of
the church dates from the
medieval or post-war periods,
following damage during the
Blitz. As well as inflicting a
lot of damage, the German
bombs revealed what is
thought to be an Anglo-
Saxon arch, made partly of
recycled Roman stonework.

The free crypt museum
in All Hallows by the
Tower also features Saxon
stonework, a 3D model of
Roman London and other
incredible artefacts.

Crowns and Christendom
(1066–1666)

FROM THE CONQUEROR TO CATASTROPHE

London's Oldest Building

What: *The White Tower*
Where: *The Tower of London, EC3N 4AB*

The oldest surviving building in London is the White Tower in the Tower of London.

Built for William the Conqueror from 1078 to 1097, it is now dwarfed by skyscrapers, but when it was built, it would have been a powerful statement of the new king's authority.

Made predominantly from Kentish ragstone, and whitewashed in 1240, which is where it gets the name 'White Tower', it was dressed and accented with Caen stone to make it abundantly clear that London was now under new, French leadership. Much of the original Caen stone was unfortunately replaced with Portland stone from the 17th century onwards.

Westminster Hall, the oldest part of the Palace of Westminster, is the second oldest, completed in 1099 for King William II, son of William the Conqueror.

> MORE PEOPLE WERE EXECUTED INSIDE THE TOWER IN THE 20TH CENTURY THAN IN ALL OTHER CENTURIES COMBINED. THIS WAS DUE TO THE EXECUTION OF SPIES AND PRISONERS DURING THE WORLD WARS.

The Ruins of a Medieval Palace

What: *Winchester Palace remains*
Where: *Pickford Wharf, SE1 9DN*

Among the winding, cobbled lanes of Bankside you'll find the ruins of one of medieval London's largest, but rather forgotten buildings: Winchester Palace.

Built in the 12th century, it was once home to the influential Bishops of Winchester. They often held powerful positions within court and significant events were known to have taken place at the palace, such as the wedding of Joan Beaufort and James I of Scotland in 1424.

The Bishop of Winchester was also able to grant licences for brothels in the area in the medieval period. The sex workers in this area were therefore known as Winchester Geese. The 'geese' part potentially comes from the goose-like noises or actions they would make to catch the attention of passers-by.

The last Bishop of Winchester to use the palace died in 1626 and most of the buildings were destroyed in a large fire in 1814. All that is left today are the ruins of the Great Hall, including its beautiful rose window.

London's Oldest Parish Church

What: *St Bartholomew the Great church*
Where: *Cloth Fair, EC1A 7JQ*

The vast majority of medieval buildings we have left are, of course, churches. If you really want to feel like you have stepped back in time, go to St Bartholomew the Great church.

Founded in 1123, it is arguably London's oldest parish church. The architecture here is a fascinating insight into changing fashions and building techniques during this period. Half of the church is built in the Romanesque style, brought over by the Normans, with rounded arches and large, stout columns. Halfway through construction, however, the Gothic style came into vogue and so the southern end has thinner columns, facilitated by the new, stronger pointed arches.

All combine to create an incredibly atmospheric space. Inside, spot the oriel window above the choir, installed in 1517, apparently so that the prior could spy on the monks.

THE LADY CHAPEL OF ST BARTHOLOMEW THE GREAT WAS USED AS A PRINTWORKS IN THE 18TH CENTURY, WHERE A YOUNG BENJAMIN FRANKLIN ONCE WORKED.

Going Gothic

What: *Gothic churches*
Where: *Westminster Abbey, SW1P 3PA;*
Southwark Cathedral, SE1 9DA

Following on from Romanesque, the predominant architectural style from the 12th to the 16th centuries was Gothic.

King Edward the Confessor had the first Westminster Abbey built in the Romanesque style from 1045 to 1050. The church was then rebuilt in the 13th century on the orders of King Henry III.

Most of the main body of Westminster Abbey today dates from the 13th and 14th centuries and is of the French Gothic style.

Notable features include the pointed arch entranceways and flying buttresses to support the extreme height of the building.

Later additions include the stunning perpendicular Gothic Lady Chapel at the southern end, added by King Henry VII and finished in 1516. The two huge Portland stone western towers were added in 1745 and designed by Nicholas Hawksmoor.

Spot the statues of 'modern martyrs' above the Great West Door added in 1995, commemorating ten modern figures persecuted or oppressed for their faith including Dr Martin Luther King.

Although much reconstructed in the 19th century, Southwark Cathedral is another beautiful example of a Gothic-style church.

St Ghastly Grim

What: St Olave's Church
Where: Hart Street, EC3R 7NA

St Olave's Church, Hart Street, was built in 1450, but there are records of a church on the site from at least the 13th century.

It is of the perpendicular Gothic style: a style popular from the middle of the 13th century until the beginning of the 16th century. It is a simpler, less frilly English adaptation of the French Gothic style that had come before it, with towers preferred over spires and a focus on straight, vertical lines. Other examples include St Andrew Undershaft church and the King's Chapel of the Savoy.

Spot the three steps down from the churchyard into the nave. You will often find medieval churches have raised churchyards due to the centuries worth of bodies underneath, particularly those used as plague burial grounds. There were over 300 victims of the Great Plague in 1665 buried at St Olave's Hart Street, with a 'p' by their names in the parish register.

Notice the memento mori symbol of three skulls over the entrance to the churchyard as well, leading Charles Dickens to dub the church 'St Ghastly Grim'.

London Bridge Is Falling Down

What: The remains of old London Bridge
Where: Victoria Park, E9 5EQ; Guy's Hospital,
SE1 9RT; Courtlands Estate, TW10 5AT; The King's
Arms, SE1 1YT; St Magnus the Martyr, EC3R 6DN

The London Bridge you see today is a pretty dull, standard concrete-and-steel construction, opened in 1973.

The medieval London Bridge that stood here from 1209–1831 however was much more impressive. Its 19 arches spanned the river roughly 30 metres (100 feet) downstream from the current London Bridge and was the first bridge to be constructed of stone in the city. By the 15th century, it was lined with houses, shops and even a chapel, treacherously teetering over the turbulent Thames below. The bridge was finally demolished in 1831, but there are a few remnants left to see.

The buildings were removed from the bridge in the 18th century to ease congestion and a balustrade and alcoves were added.

You can see two of these alcoves in Victoria Park, another in the grounds of Guy's Hospital and one in Courtlands Estate in Richmond.

You can also see a coat of arms, dating from 1730, that once adorned the southern gateway, on the front of The King's Arms pub in Southwark.

There are also some old stones from the medieval London Bridge in the churchyard of St Magnus the Martyr church. The tower once formed a pedestrian entrance to the old London Bridge and inside the church you can find an amazing 3D model of what it would have looked like.

Tudor Treasures

What: St Bartholomew's Gatehouse
Where: Smithfield, EC1A 9DS

When you think of Tudor architecture, your mind probably jumps to the classic black-and-white timber-framed buildings. For a beautiful example, see St Bartholomew's Gatehouse in Smithfield. Built in 1595, it sits on top of a 13th-century archway that, before the Dissolution of the Monasteries, formed the entrance to the southern nave of St Bartholomew the Great church behind.

Shockingly, the facade was covered up during the Georgian period and only rediscovered when a bomb from a Zeppelin raid in 1917 exposed the Tudor delight underneath.

A Remarkable Survivor

What: *The oldest house in the City of London*
Where: *41–42 Cloth Fair, EC1A 7JQ*

Hidden among the warren of medieval alleyways in Smithfield you will find the City of London's oldest purpose-built house. Made from brick and timber and completed in 1614, this beautiful building has remarkably survived the Great Fire (it was protected by the priory walls of St Bartholomew the Great church), the Blitz and overzealous developers.

Scheduled for demolition in 1929, it was thankfully saved when the architects Paul Paget and John Seely restored the building to use as their office.

Among those who are said to have visited the house are Sir Winston Churchill and the Queen Mother who, as was the tradition of the time, carved their names into an upper-floor window with a diamond pen.

Spot the pedimented, rectangular, timbered bay windows with leaded glass, transporting you back to Jacobean London.

Getting Thrown Out

What: *Overhanging jetties*
Where: *229 Strand, WC2R 1BF*

Despite its unassuming appearance, 229 Strand is a very rare pre-Great Fire of London survivor, thought to have been built around 1630.

A clue is the projecting upper floor: a practice known as jettying. You will notice 229 and its neighbour 230, a late-17th-century building, are very narrow, as the frontage onto the busy thoroughfare was expensive. Jettying was therefore a popular way to maximise space.

Jettying, however, enabled fires to spread more quickly as the buildings on either side of the narrow lanes were practically leaning into each other and sometimes almost touching. In fact, some medieval streets, including London Bridge at points, were said to feel like tunnels, with all the light blocked by overhanging jetties. The structures were therefore banned in the slew of building regulations following the Great Fire of London.

The word 'jetty' comes from the French word *jeter* meaning 'to throw'. 'Jettison' also has the same etymology.

The Age of Wren

What: *Christopher Wren's churches*
Where: *St Stephen Walbrook, EC4N 8BN; St Benet Paul's Wharf, EC4V 4ER; St James Garlickhythe, EC4V 2AF*

Probably more than anyone else, the architect who has left his mark on London is Sir Christopher Wren. He designed all manner of buildings but is best known for his churches. Out of the 107 parish churches in the City of London, 85 were destroyed during the Great Fire in 1666. Wren was commissioned to reconstruct 51 of them and his masterpiece: St Paul's Cathedral.

Wren usually had to work within the footprint of the original church and sometimes would try to incorporate elements from them in his design.

Therefore, every Wren church is different, but there are a couple of reasonably common features to look out for:

- Wren generally used a pared-back Baroque style, less frilly than the European Baroque counterpart, combined with classical and occasional Gothic features.
- A square or rectangular tower at the west side, topped by a unique spire.
- Portland stone structures but occasionally red brick with stone dressings.
- White-washed ceilings and walls.
- Generally clear windows rather than stained glass to create brighter interiors.

The Wedding Cake Church

What: St Bride's Church
Where: Fleet Street, EC4Y 8AU

One of the most spectacular of Wren's spires is that of St Bride's Church, just off Fleet Street.

The medieval church was destroyed in the Great Fire and a new church was built to Wren's designs in 1675.

Constructed in 1703, the five-tiered, 70-metre (226-feet) spire was Wren's tallest and is said to have inspired the design for the modern tiered wedding cake. The story goes that William Rich, a baker's apprentice who worked in nearby Ludgate Circus, fell in love with his master's daughter. He proposed to her and, wanting to impress both father and daughter, set out to create a magnificent wedding cake. Casting his eyes around for inspiration, he saw the spire of St Bride's and thus was born the tiered wedding cake.

During the 16th and 17th centuries a 'bride pie' would have been served to the wedding guests. One particular recipe from 1685 included oysters, lamb's testicles, pine kernels and cock's combs, as well as a compartment for either live birds or a snake to burst out and surprise the hungry crowd.

London's Oldest Pub?

What: Ye Olde Cheshire Cheese
Where: Fleet Street, EC4A 2BP

Now, there are a number of pubs with a claim to being London's oldest; some more dubious than others.

Certainly one of London's oldest is Ye Olde Cheshire Cheese on Fleet Street. It was originally built in 1530 but burnt down in the Great Fire in 1666. Londoners do not like to be without their pubs, so it was rebuilt very soon after, in 1667. On the outside it displays the names of all the monarchs' reigns that it has been open for, starting from Charles II.

Although it has been 'very much altered', the vaulted cellars beneath, in which you can drink your pint, are thought to be original. Some sources even claim that these are part of an old 13th-century Carmelite monastery, but this seems highly unlikely.

London's Last Galleried Coaching Inn

What: The George Inn
Where: Borough High Street, SE1 1NH

Walk down the cobbled entranceway off Borough High Street to The George Inn and you will feel as if you have been transported back to 17th-century London.

There has been an inn on the site since at least the 16th century, but the current building dates from 1676 and is London's last remaining galleried coaching inn.

London was once full of coaching inns: termini for stagecoach companies transporting people all over the country. Borough High Street was once an important route out of London to the south, particularly to Canterbury for pilgrimages, as seen in Geoffrey Chaucer's *The Canterbury Tales*.

Back to the Classics

What: *Palladian architecture*
Where: *Banqueting House, SW1A 2ER*

From the early 17th century onwards, we see the arrival of Palladian architecture. The name came from the Italian architect Andrea Palladio (1508–80) and was inspired by the architecture of ancient Greece and Rome, championing symmetry and proportion.

Built from 1619–22, the Banqueting House on Whitehall is all that is left of what was once a sprawling royal palace. Whitehall Palace was originally the home of the Archbishop of York but was taken from Cardinal Wolsey by King Henry VIII.

The Banqueting House was designed by Inigo Jones and is one of the first examples of the principles of Palladianism being used on an English building. Spot the sharp focus on symmetry and classical decorations, such as pediments over the windows, Ionic columns and Corinthian pilasters. Around the top of the building is a frieze of carved garlands and masks, pointing to the building's original purpose as a venue for balls and performances.

Over the entranceway is a bust of King Charles I: a nod to the fact that it was on a scaffold outside Banqueting House that he was executed on the 30th January 1649.

A Forbidden Chapel

What: *The Queen's Chapel*
Where: *Marlborough Road, SW1A 1BG*

Next to St James's Palace you will find another of Inigo Jones' works: the demure Queen's Chapel.

Built from 1623–25, it was constructed for Queen Henrietta Maria, the Roman Catholic wife of King Charles I, at a time when Roman Catholic churches were otherwise forbidden. It was the first classical-style church in England and so a highly significant building architecturally. Notice the simple, proportional rectangular shape and classical features, such as the pedimented ends and arched window.

Another example of a church by Inigo Jones is St Paul's Covent Garden, completed in 1633. Its famous portico and Tuscan columns face onto the Covent Garden piazza, also laid out by Jones in the style of Italian squares.

The large eastern door facing onto the piazza is, in fact, a fake. Inigo Jones originally intended it to be the front door to the church but this went against the Christian tradition of the altar being placed at the eastern end of the church. The entrances therefore had to be reversed, leaving the Great East door as a dummy.

High Society Living

What: *Garden squares*
Where: *Bedford Square, WC1B 3RB*

A defining feature of London's landscape is the garden square.

In the 16th and 17th centuries, London began to spread outside the traditional confines of the city walls. The Great Fire in 1666 destroyed over 13,000 homes in the old medieval city and turbo-charged this change.

The aristocrats who had benefitted from Henry VIII's seizing of church lands during the Dissolution of the Monasteries also took advantage of this shift and started building grand squares of townhouses around pleasant gardens. This was partly to maintain green space in the city and partly inspired by the design of Italian piazzas, with a classical style of architecture and town planning taking hold.

At first they were specifically aimed at an upper-class clientele; for example, Covent Garden in 1631 was designed by Inigo Jones for the Duke of Bedford and Bloomsbury Square was developed in the early 1660s for the Earl of Southampton. Laid out from 1775–83, Bedford Square in Bloomsbury is one of London's best-preserved Georgian garden squares.

The Oldest Terraced Houses in London

What: Terraced housing from 17th–18th centuries
Where: 52–55 Newington Green, N16 9PX

After the Great Fire of London, the vogue was for uniform, terraced housing.

Building regulations became far more standardised with the Rebuilding of London Act 1666 and subsequent acts. Houses were to be built of brick or stone, overhanging jetties were banned and standardised heights and styles were encouraged.

Terraced housing therefore proliferated, predominantly now as homes for the growing merchant/industrial middle classes rather than for the rich and wealthy. The style of the new terraces took inspiration from Palladianism and classical architecture, championing order, logicality and proportion.

You can see a couple of examples of original 17th-century terraces with few alterations on Essex Street, but for the oldest terraced houses in London, you will need to go to 52–55 Newington Green, built in 1658.

A Window into the Past

What: Sash windows
Where: Cowley Street, SW1P 3LZ

Sash windows were introduced to Britain towards the end of the 17th century, probably from Holland or France. The sash, as opposed to the casement window, which opened outwards, meant that, when it was opened, the symmetry of the classical facade was not compromised.

In 1709 an act was introduced stating that sash windows must be recessed 4 inches (10 centimetres) back from the outer

masonry (although there was generally a slow uptake of this) and a further act of 1774 stating that the ropes and pulley mechanism must be concealed behind masonry as a fire precaution. Walk from 9 Smith Square to 17 Cowley Street in Westminster and you can admire a variety of recessed and unrecessed 18th-century sash windows.

Another feature to look for are the number of panes. With large panes of glass difficult and expensive to produce, the 12-pane sash window is an archetypal Georgian feature. As time went on, panes increased in size, so in the Victorian period 2- or 4-pane windows were most common.

lack of ventilation and light having significant negative effects on health and wellbeing. At the same time, many of the wealthy simply avoided the tax by bricking over a few of their windows. The ineffective and damaging tax was only finally repealed in 1851.

It is worth saying that most bricked-up or covered windows are not a result of the window tax. Architects often use 'dummy' windows to maintain proportion or symmetry on a building. For a window tax culprit, look for a lack of symmetry or mismatching bricks. There are a couple of potential, but unconfirmed, examples of window tax avoidance at 25 Eccleston Street and between 49–52 Chiswell Street.

Daylight Robbery

What: *Bricked-up windows*
Where: *25 Eccleston Street, SW1W 9NP;*
49–52 Chiswell Street, EC1Y 4SA

In 1696 one of Britain's most notorious taxes was introduced: the window tax. The idea was that the more windows you had, the richer you were, and so the more tax you would pay. The tax was initially imposed if you had more than 10 windows. As with all well-laid plans however, it did not quite work out like that.

Firstly, the poorest in the city often lived together in tenement buildings with lots of windows. The landlords, therefore, raised the rent to pay the tax or simply blocked the windows. When new tenement buildings were constructed, the number of windows were kept to a minimum with the

Size Matters

What: *Georgian windows*
Where: *36 Craven Street, WC2N 5NF*

An architectural clue to help denote the age of a building is the size of its window.

In the late 17th century, townhouses would generally have the same sized windows at ground and first floor levels. As you move into the 18th century, a general rule of thumb is that the windows tend to get smaller as you go up the building. Ground and first floor rooms were for the homeowners, with the upper floors more likely to be occupied by servants.

However, in the early 18th century, a fashion developed in some circles to have the main entertaining space on the first floor, and so houses built in this period often have larger first floor windows and became known as the *piano nobile* or 'noble floor'. A good example of this can be found at 36 Craven Street, where Benjamin Franklin lived for 16 years.

In the late 18th century, the trend was reversed and the ground floor was predominantly used again for entertaining.

In the early 19th century, two-window-wide houses often widened the single ground floor window for more light, meaning that the door was pushed slightly to one side. This compromised the symmetry of the building but marked a move towards functionality over aesthetics.

Snuffed Out

What: Torch snuffers or 'link extinguishers'
Where: 18 and 19 Curzon Street, W1J 7TA;
26 Queen Anne's Gate, SW1H 9AB

Before widespread street lighting, Londoners were somewhat left to their own devices when it came to finding their way at night.

The wealthy often had servants to carry their torches for them through the city or you could hire a 'link-boy' to walk in front of you to your home. A link-boy was essentially a young, poor street urchin, armed with a homemade torch. In order to snuff out the torch, conical iron devices were installed on the outside of houses to extinguish the flame.

You would have been wise to be wary however as these link-boys were notorious for working with local criminal gangs to lead their unwitting charges down dangerous alleyways to be mugged or worse.

Getting Stoned

What: *Coade stone*
Where: *Bedford Square, WC1B 3RB; Queen Anne's Gate, SW1H 9BU; Westminster Bridge, SE1 7GA*

The 18th century saw the arrival of a new transformative artificial stone known as Coade stone.

Made from clay, terracotta, silicates and glass, the secret recipe was refined and improved in the 1770s by a formidable businesswoman called Eleanor Coade. Produced from a factory in Lambeth, Coade stone was very durable and could be easily cast into intricate shapes, perfect for architectural decoration and sculpture. The 1774 building act required that new houses did not have any wooden decoration and so, instead, builders turned to Coade stone.

Eleanor Coade died in 1821 and without her leadership the business closed in the 1840s. The recipe was lost right up until the 1990s when someone managed to recreate it, but you can still see Coade stone all over the city – it has a smooth, usually pristine, white appearance – for example, the Coade stone masks above the entranceways of the houses on Bedford Square and Queen Anne's Gate. It was also used for some statues and sculptures, for example the South Bank Lion next to Westminster Bridge.

Casting Around for a Solution

What: *Cast-iron shoe scrapers*
Where: *11–13 Chesterfield Street, W1J 5JN*

The arrival of the steam engine in the 18th century meant that cast-iron production methods were improved and greater uniformity could be achieved at a lower cost.

Cast-iron railings and decorative balconies became very popular, as well as other accessories, such as the humble shoe scraper, or the rather classier French term for them: a *décrottoir*. As paving and public spaces were improved in the 18th and 19th centuries, the wealthy were more inclined to perambulate around London and therefore shoe scrapers for removing the unwanted deposits from the city were required at the entrances to their townhouses. The townhouses of Mayfair are great locations for spotting these, with a prime example being the houses at 11–13 Chesterfield Street.

Functional Fenestration

What: *Fanlights*
Where: *10 Downing Street, SW1A 2AB*

From around the 1720s, a common feature of the terraced house was a fanlight above the front door. These usually semi-circular, fan-shaped windows were intended to allow light into otherwise windowless hallways.

Over time they became more intricate with improvements to metal-work processes and as architectural decoration became more lavish.

A fanlight can be seen on London's most famous Georgian property: 10 Downing Street.

The Fake 10 Downing Street

What: *10 Adam Street*
Where: *WC2R 0DE*

Have you ever wanted a photo in front of 10 Downing Street and do not happen to be a visiting dignitary? Well then, head to 10 Adam Street instead.

Built from 1768–74, with its black bricks, cream-coloured door surround, fanlight and black cast-iron railings, number 10 Adam Street looks remarkably like the famous home of the Prime Minister.

Both houses have the characteristic black-painted bricks, but this was not always the case. The bricks at 10 Downing Street were cleaned in the 1950s, revealing that they were, in fact, yellow, the black being the result of centuries of pollution.

The yellow, it was thought, did not look prime-ministerial enough and so the black paint came out and it was returned to its previous appearance.

An A-mews-ing Interlude

What: *Mews streets*
Where: *Eccleston Mews, SW1X 8AG;*
Kynance Mews, SW7 4QP

Behind the grander terraces of townhouses for the upper classes in Mayfair, Kensington and Belgravia, for example, you will find narrower, often cobbled, service roads for stabling, servants' quarters and later, garages, known as a 'mews'.

The origin of the name 'mews' goes back to the late 14th century when the King kept his royal hunting hawks at Charing Cross. 'Mew' originally referred to a hawk's moulting period, when it could not be flown and was kept caged. Over time it came to refer to the cages themselves and the Charing Cross site became known as the King's Mews. The site was rebuilt as stables in 1534 following a fire, but the name stuck. George IV moved the royal stables to Buckingham Palace in the early 19th century and Trafalgar Square was laid out on the site.

Therefore, when the new service roads for stabling were laid out behind grand townhouses, they also took on the 'mews' name.

AT AROUND 7.25 ACRES, THE LARGEST PUBLIC SQUARE IN LONDON IS LINCOLN'S INN FIELDS. IT WAS LAID OUT IN THE 1630S AND TAKES ITS NAME FROM THE ADJACENT LINCOLN'S INN, ONE OF THE INNS OF COURT.

London's Smallest Square

What: *Pickering Place*
Where: *St James's Street, SW1A 1EA*

Walk down the dark, covered passageway next to Berry Bros & Rudd in St James's and you will find a lovely surprise: London's smallest public square.

Dating from the 1730s, Pickering Place is a beautiful little time capsule, transporting you back to Georgian London.

It may seem peaceful now, but its secluded location meant that it was initially infamous for its gambling dens and duels. Urban myth has it that the last-ever duel in England took place here in the 19th century.

Make sure to spot the plaque at the entrance highlighting that the Texan Legation (essentially the embassy) was based here from 1842–1845, before Texas joined the USA.

Me-sphinx I Am in Egypt

What: Sphinx sculptures
Where: Richmond Avenue, N1 0NA

Richmond Avenue in Islington is a lovely
but fairly standard, leafy north London
street. Look again at some of the houses,
however, and you'll notice that they are
being guarded by Egyptian sphinxes.
In 1798 a French invasion force under the
command of Napoleon disembarked in
Egypt. Accompanying them were scholars
and scientists ready to study Egyptian
culture and civilisation. It was at this time

that the Rosetta Stone, now in the British
Museum, was discovered.

A month after the French arrived, a
British fleet under the command of Lord
Horatio Nelson obliterated the French
fleet at anchor, thus stranding the French
army in Egypt. It was a key juncture in the
Napoleonic Wars.

Following Nelson's victory there was
a burst of enthusiasm in Britain for all
things Egyptian. In 1841 the sphinxes and
obelisks, with 'NILE' inscribed onto them
were installed on Richmond Avenue by the
surveyor of the Thornhill Estate, Joseph Kay,
when the houses were being constructed.

Stucco in a Rut

What: *Stucco*
Where: *Belgrave Square, SW1X 8NT;*
Cumberland Terrace, NW1 4HS

In certain areas of London, you will find an abundance of buildings clad in a gleaming cream- or white-coloured stucco rendering.

In the late 18th century, stucco began to be used to render the ground floor of buildings. In the Regency and early Victorian periods, it became increasingly popular to completely render the house or terrace, for smooth, evenly coloured facades. Made from lime mortar mixed with other materials, it covered the underlying masonry and had the appearance of stone while being very cheap to produce.

The great Regency architects John Nash and Thomas Cubitt were keen proponents of stucco. Thomas Cubitt is most well known for his commission from Richard Grosvenor, Marquess of Westminster, to create housing on his estates in Belgravia and Pimlico in the 1820s. Walk around these areas today, for example Belgrave Square, and you will see that it is all still pretty much intact.

John Nash designed the stunning stucco-clad villas and grand neo-classical terraces around Regent's Park, such as Cumberland Terrace. Completed in 1826, he used features from ancient Greek temples, including triumphal arches linking the blocks, a huge pediment over a colonnade of Ionic columns and sculptures of mythical figures.

Shop 'Til You Drop

What: *Georgian shops*
Where: *88 Dean Street, W1D 3ST; 56 Artillery Lane, E1 7LS; Woburn Walk; WC1H 0JJ*

As the middle class started to grow in the 18th century, so did the desire for shopping. Sadly, there are not many authentic Georgian shopfronts left in London but that makes the ones we do have all the more precious.

They are characterised by bay windows made up of small panes of glass for displaying goods. A beautiful example of a Georgian shopfront can be seen at 88 Dean Street. Dating from 1791 and Grade II listed, the building has a painted wooden front and two large bay windows. Other examples can be found at 56 Artillery Lane and on Woburn Walk.

THE NAME ARTILLERY LANE AND THE NEARBY ARTILLERY PASSAGE BOTH COME FROM THE FACT THAT THIS AREA WAS, DURING THE REIGN OF KING HENRY VIII, TURNED INTO A MILITARY TRAINING GROUND, PARTICULARLY FOR ARTILLERY, CROSSBOWS AND LONGBOWS.

A Watchful Eye

What: *Watchhouses*
Where: *St Mary Rotherhithe, SE16 4JE; St Mary Magdalen Bermondsey, SE1 3UW*

A rather ominous feature that occasionally accompanied cemeteries in the 18th and 19th centuries were watchhouses.

In the late 18th century, a growth in the medical profession led to an increase in the demand for human bodies for anatomical study. Prior to the Anatomy Act of 1832, only the bodies of those executed for crimes could be used for such purposes. The number of executions was, however, falling, creating a gap between supply and demand.

As ever with London, an enterprising character was willing to fill that gap.

Body snatchers, or 'resurrectionists', engaged in the grisly business of covertly digging up fresh corpses from graveyards to sell to anatomists.

A number of measures were implemented to deter them; for example, iron coffins that were harder to be broken into (you can see one in the crypt of St Bride's Church) and 'mortsafes', essentially cages for coffins.

Another feature were watchhouses: usually small, simple one- or two-storey buildings by the entrance to the cemetery, for wardens to keep an eye from. You can find surviving examples at St Mary Rotherhithe and another in Bermondsey next to the St Mary Magdalen churchyard, both dating from around the 1820s.

The Imperial City
(1837–1914)

THE GREAT CITY TO THE GREAT WAR

Catering for the Masses

What: *The Victorian terrace*
Where: *Ladbroke Gardens, W11 2PT; Fentiman Road, SW8 1JY; Croftdown Road, NW5 1EN; Groombridge Road, E9 7DH*

Victorian London saw massive population growth from roughly one million in 1800 to around six million in 1900. This, of course, led to a need for new homes and the terraced house was still the go-to model. The arrival of the railways in the mid-19th century precipitated the huge expansion of the city into what was once countryside, meaning that most of the buildings you see outside the centre are Victorian terraces.

Victorian terraced houses generally had some extra features, compared to their Georgian counterparts, for example porches and bay windows. Windowpanes were usually larger due to the invention of rolled plate glass in 1847, with a two-over-two-pane window the most common.

The plain brick of the 18th century or stucco of the early 19th century were often replaced with coloured brickwork and terracotta as the century went on. Other common features to look out for are a more elaborate gable trim, a high-pitched roof and Gothic features such as stained glass, towers or turrets.

LONDON WAS THE CITY WITH THE LARGEST POPULATION IN THE WORLD FROM THE LATE 1820S UNTIL THE 1920S.

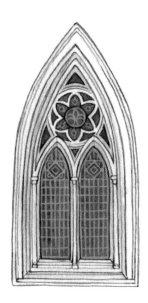

A Gothic Resurrection

What: *Gothic revival architecture*
Where: *The Houses of Parliament, SW1A 0AA;*
All Saints Margaret Street, W1W 8JG; St Pancras
Renaissance Hotel, NW1 2AR; Royal Courts of
Justice, WC2A 2LL

The Victorian period also heralded the
return of Gothic architecture. This style
countered the symmetry and order of
classical architecture, instead championing
individualism, elaborate decoration and a
return to what was seen as a more Christian
and inherently English style of architecture.

When the Houses of Parliament
burnt down in 1834, a new building was
required, and it was felt that it needed to
complement the Gothic architecture of
Westminster Abbey. The new Gothic-style
Houses of Parliament were designed by
classical architect Sir Charles Barry with
the assistance of Gothic Revival pioneer
Augustus Pugin.

We, therefore, see the return of
pointed arches, very narrow lancet windows
and gargoyles among other features.
The Gothic Revival movement can be seen
all over London in religious buildings, such
as All Saints Margaret Street, and secular
buildings, such as St Pancras Renaissance
Hotel and the Royal Courts of Justice.

A Gothic Hidden Gem

What: Two Temple Place
Where: Temple, WC2R 3BD

A beautiful example of a neo-Gothic building is Two Temple Place, just off the Victoria Embankment.

Constructed in 1895 and designed by John Loughborough Pearson, it was built for William Waldorf Astor, probably the richest man in the world at the time, best known for establishing the Waldorf Astoria hotels.

Made of Portland stone and complete with crenellations, stained-glass windows and intricate stone carvings, it looks like it has been transported out of an old English gothic fantasy-world.

Make sure to spot the green lampposts outside the front entrance. Look closely and you will notice that the cherubs at the base are on the telephone. Two Temple Place was one of the first buildings in London to have a telephone and William Waldorf Astor was keen to show off this fact.

Also before you go, admire the magnificent golden weathervane in the form of the *Santa María,* the ship Christopher Columbus sailed to America.

Temples of Intemperance

What: The Victorian pub
Where: Prince Albert, NW1 0SG; Lord Clyde, SE1 1ER; The Three Crowns, N1 6AD

At the corner of a 19th century terrace can often be found a Victorian pub. Corners, with their double road frontage and larger square footage, were usually built specifically to be pubs.

A significant 'temperance' movement was underway in the 19th century, encouraging moderation and abstinence from alcohol, so the pubs felt they needed to change their image somewhat. In the late Victorian and Edwardian periods therefore, pubs went from slightly dark and dingy establishments to extravagantly decorated, eye-catching architectural gems.

Breweries, many of whom rebuilt pubs at the turn of the 19th century, used this as an opportunity to advertise their brand name, for example Charrington Brewery, Barclay, Perkins & Co or the Truman Brewery.

Glass Distinctions

What: Saloon bars and 'snob screens'
Where: The Blackfriar, EC4V 4EG; The Lamb, WC1N 3LZ

Class distinctions were very important to the Victorians, and this did not stop at the pub door. Many 19th-century pubs had a separate saloon bar for wealthier patrons. A surviving example can be seen at The Blackfriar pub.

Glass screens, aka 'snob screens', were also introduced in some establishments to shield the upper-class customers from views of hoi polloi at the main bar. You can still see one of these at the The Lamb pub in Holborn.

A Turkish Delight

What: A Victorian Turkish bath house
Where: 7–8 Bishopsgate Churchyard, EC2M 3TJ

Turn down a side-alley off bustling Bishopsgate and you will find something rather surprising: an ornate Victorian Turkish bath house that looks like it has been transported directly out of the Middle East.

There has been a bath house on the site since 1817, with this incarnation being constructed in 1895. Turkish bath houses, essentially saunas that used hot air instead of steam, became popular in the second half of the 19th century, among those with sufficient disposable income. At the height of their popularity, there were over one hundred in London.

The shape of the building is modelled on the Church of the Holy Sepulchre in Jerusalem and the outside is bedecked in coloured tiles, stained glass and intricate carved stonework. It closed as a bath house in 1954 and today is a restaurant and events space.

Tiles for Trains

What: *Oxblood-tile Underground stations*
Where: *Covent Garden, WC2E 9JT;*
Russell Square Station, WC1N 1HX

Of the 272 Underground stations in London, the most iconic are those with the distinctive red, or oxblood, coloured, glazed terracotta tiles. They were designed by Leslie Green who, in 1903, was appointed by the Underground Electric Railways Company of London to design 50 stations, including Covent Garden and Russell Square.

They are generally two-storey buildings with large arched windows

and a flat roof to encourage upper-storey development. In 1907 the stress of the project took its toll on Green's health and he had to retire. He sadly died just a year later at the age of 33.

Kilburn Park, Maida Vale and the Bakerloo line entrance to Paddington were all constructed after his death but using the same design principles.

Ghost Platforms

What: *Abandoned railway stations*
Where: *Down Street station, W1J 7JU;*
Aldwych station, WC2R 2NE

Occasionally on London's streets you will stumble upon an abandoned railway station. Stations were usually closed when they were no longer financially viable to keep open but often went on to serve other uses.

Down Street station opened in 1907 as part of the Great Northern, Piccadilly and Brompton Railway. However, with Hyde Park Corner and Green Park nearby, it closed in 1932 due to low passenger numbers. It found a new lease of life during World War Two, however, when it was used as the headquarters of the Railway Executive Committee and then as the base for Churchill's war cabinet

before the Cabinet War Rooms were constructed underneath Whitehall.

Opened in 1907, Aldwych on Strand was similarly used during the war. The British Museum used the tunnel between Aldwych and Holborn to keep the Elgin Marbles safe from enemy bombing. The station itself only shut in 1994, being the only station on a separate spur of the Piccadilly Line.

The stations are still occasionally used for filming and Transport for London run occasional tours of them.

A Cheeky Half

What: *The Wheatsheaf*
Where: *6 Stoney Street, SE1 9AA*

The arrival of the railways in the mid-19th century transformed the city. Not only could London expand and take over more of the surrounding countryside but railways also affected the physical landscape of the city with huge stations and railways lines carving their way through the streets. This often left individual or small groups of houses cut adrift, so look out for these by railway lines.

An interesting 20th-century variation of this can be found in Borough Market. The Wheatsheaf pub opened in the 1770s and was rebuilt in 1840 as a three-storey building. However, in 2009, the pub had to be shut for four years while the top floor was totally removed for a viaduct of the Thameslink programme.

The Railway of Death

What: *The London Necropolis Railway*
Where: *121 Westminster Bridge Road, SE1 7HR*

By the middle of the 19th century, London's inner-city graveyards were full.

Private businesses, with the encouragement of the state, stepped in to help solve this problem. In 1852 the London Necropolis Company established the brand-new Brookwood cemetery in Surrey, the world's largest at the time. So far, so good.

The next issue was how to get the dead and their mourners out there. Enter the Necropolis Railway. A railway service specifically for this purpose, the London Necropolis Railway had termini at Brookwood and Waterloo, spurred off the main train lines. It had its own rolling stock and, at its peak, transported 2,000 (dead) bodies a year to Brookwood. It eventually closed in 1941 due to lower-than-expected profits and wartime damage.

The only reminder of this railway for the dead in London is at 121 Westminster Bridge Road. Dating from 1901, this building was the first-class entrance. First-class passengers enjoyed a fancier arrival, more luxurious carriages, were allowed to witness the coffins being loaded onto the trains and could pick where the coffin was buried in the cemetery. In true Victorian style, not only were the living separated by class, the dead were too, with separate carriages for first-, second- and third-class coffins.

Cannon Cradling

What: *Imperial Edwardian architecture*
Where: *Admiralty Arch, SW1A 2WH*

At the beginning of the 20th century, London was the world's largest city and the heart of the world's largest empire. European powers were scrabbling for more territory around the world and building up their militaries.

Out of this environment came the neo-Baroque architecture of the Edwardian period, aiming to show off Britain's imperial might. The style evokes the classical empires with features such as columns, pediments and pyramidal sculpture groups, while also harking back to the monumental Baroque works of Sir Christopher Wren.

Examples include Australia House and the War Office building on Whitehall, but one of the most striking examples is Admiralty Arch by Trafalgar Square. It was designed as an office space for the admiralty but also as a powerful piece of statement architecture. Opened in 1912, it was designed by Aston Webb, also responsible for the eastern facade of Buckingham Palace and the Victoria Memorial. The aim was for this to be a part of an imperial, processional route from Buckingham Palace to St Paul's Cathedral.

Spot the two sculptural figures on the western side by Thomas Brock, depicting *Navigation* and *Gunnery*. You'll notice that the lady depicted in the *Gunnery* statue is lovingly cradling a cannon.

Glitz and Glamour

What: *Art-deco architecture*
Where: *Old Daily Telegraph Building, EC4A 2BJ; Hoover Building, UB6 8AT; Daimler Car Hire Garage, WC1N 1EX*

The art-deco style flourished in Europe in the 1920s and 1930s. The bold geometric shapes, sleek lines, bright colours and curved elements all came together to symbolise decadence, luxury and modernity.

The stunning Daily Telegraph Building on Fleet Street, opened in 1928, has a combination of classical features, such as the colonnade of Doric columns and art-deco features, including the beautiful, colourful clock, added in 1930.

Other, more pure art-deco examples are the Hoover Building in Ealing (1932) and the Daimler Car Hire Garage building in Bloomsbury (1931).

AUSTRALIA HOUSE, THE AUSTRALIAN HIGH COMMISSION, WAS CONSTRUCTED IN 1918 AND IS THE LONGEST OCCUPIED DIPLOMATIC MISSION IN THE COUNTRY. THE CENTRAL HALL WAS USED IN THE *HARRY POTTER* FILMS AS THE INTERIOR OF GRINGOTTS BANK.

The Black Cats of Mornington Crescent

What: Egypt-mania inspired architecture
Where: Carreras Cigarette Factory, NW1 7AW; Old Carlton Cinema, N1 2SN

Opened in 1928, the old Carreras Cigarette Factory is one of London's most bizarre buildings.

Influenced by Howard Carter's discovery of Tutankhamun's tomb in 1922, art-deco buildings often incorporated Egyptian-inspired features. The factory is said to be based on the Egyptian Temple of Bubastis, an ancient cat-headed goddess, but the company's logo was also handily a black cat. The entrance is therefore guarded by two huge black cat statues and black cat faces adorn the facade. Other features include the colourful decorated columns and the name of the company carved in stone. The building's opening ceremony even included chariot races in the road outside. Today it is an office building called Greater London House.

Another example of a building inspired by Egypt-mania of the 1920s and 1930s is the old Carlton Cinema on Essex Road (1930).

War and Resurgence
(1914–)

War Paint

What: *World War Two camouflage paint*
Where: *Stoke Newington Town Hall, N16 0JR*

Stoke Newington Town Hall was built between 1935–37. During World War Two the council were concerned that their new, pristine building would be used as a landmark for navigation purposes by German bombers and so camouflage paint was applied to the exterior of the building.

The building remarkably escaped the war pretty much unscathed and the camouflage paint, although faint at points, can still be seen to this day.

Taking Shelter

What: *Deep-level shelters*
Where: *79–80 Tottenham Court Road, W1T 4TD; 13 Chenies Street, WC1E 7EY*

During the Blitz, from September 1940 to May 1941, many Londoners sought shelter in the Underground railway network.

With further attacks anticipated, the British government commissioned a series of deep-level shelters across London to protect civilians. Eight were constructed, with each being able to hold up to 8,000 people, and included facilities such as toilets, bunk beds and canteens.

By the time they were finished in 1942, air raids had significantly lessened and they were mostly used for military storage and staff accommodation; however, five were used during the V1 and V2 rocket air raids from 1944–45.

Located along the Northern Line, each has two entrances that are generally circular, windowless structures constructed from brick and concrete. The entrances to the shelter near Goodge Street station are the most centrally located: on Tottenham Court Road and Chenies Street. The Chenies Street shelter (pictured below) is known as the Eisenhower Centre and was used as a headquarters for the Allied forces towards the end of the war. Today it is used for the storage of documents.

Secret Wartime Bunker

What: *Admiralty Citadel*
Where: *Horse Guards Parade, SW1A 2AX*

By Horse Guards Parade you will see a Brutalist windowless structure known as Admiralty Citadel. Despite it rather standing out from its surroundings, this was, bizarrely to the modern observer, intended as a secret bunker.

Described by Sir Winston Churchill as a 'vast monstrosity', Admiralty Citadel was constructed from 1940–41 as a bomb-proof bunker to act as the command centre for the admiralty. It has 9-metre (30-feet)-deep foundations, a 6-metre (20-feet)-thick concrete roof, tunnels linking it to Whitehall and is fitted with loop-holed gun emplacements to be used in the event of a land invasion.

Secrecy was paramount during its construction and, at first, the press was not even allowed to even acknowledge its existence. It is still used today by the Ministry of Defence and, as the ivy covering the outside changes colour through the seasons, it can be strangely beautiful.

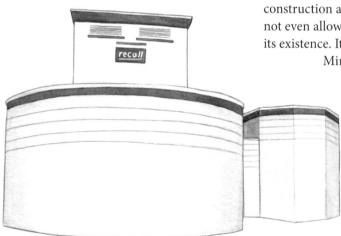

recall

The Odd One Out

What: *Post-war, high-density housing blocks*
Where: *22–26 Ovington Square, SW3 1LR;*
9–11 Cromwell Road, SW7 2JA

Walk London's streets and, in some cases, you can almost read the city's architecture like a map of where bombs landed. In historic 18th- or 19th-century areas of London you may suddenly come across an otherwise discordant post-war housing block, constructed after the war on a bombsite.

This becomes more apparent when you are admiring the gleaming, stuccoed 19th-century townhouses of West London where bombing was relatively less severe and you come across a modernist high-density housing block stuck in the middle of a terrace.

Battle Scars

What: *Shrapnel damage*
Where: *Cleopatra's Needle, WC2N 6PB;*
The Victoria and Albert Museum, SW7 2RL;
Tate Britain, SW1P 4RG; Chamber Street, E1 8AP

It is estimated that over 12,000 metric tonnes of bombs were dropped on London during World War Two and the city is not short of battle scars.

Look out for the characteristic pock-marked stone that usually signifies shrapnel damage from a World War Two bomb or even, in some cases, a World War One

Zeppelin or aeroplane air raid, such as at Cleopatra's Needle. It tends to be the sturdier buildings made of materials such as Portland stone that still display the damage, for example, the V&A and Tate Britain.

The East End was extremely badly hit, with whole areas, such as Stepney, having to be practically rebuilt from scratch after the war. Very little shrapnel damage remains in the East End because it was generally ordinary people's homes or industrial buildings that were damaged and were not restored or protected to the same degree. There is, however, a very rare example of East End shrapnel damage at the corner of Chamber Street and Mansell Street.

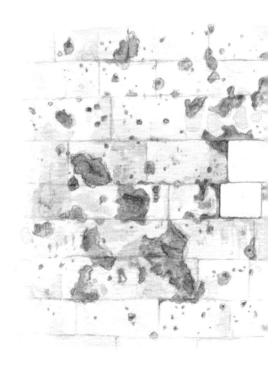

A Concrete Altar

What: St Paul's Bow Common
Where: Burdett Road, E3 4AR

After the horror of World War Two, decisions had to be made about how London was to be rebuilt. It was seen that London needed to lead the way to a bright, peaceful, utopian future. Brutalist architecture was one of the most striking products of this environment. It was seen as functional, socialist and a reaction against the frillier styles popular at the beginning of the 20th century. This can be seen in housing, such as the Barbican Estate and Trellick Tower, but also public buildings, such as the National Theatre and the Southbank Centre.

Unusually, in Tower Hamlets you find a Brutalist church. Built on the site of its Victorian predecessor, lost during the Blitz, St Paul's Bow Common was completed in 1960 and designed by architects Robert Maguire and Keith Murray. The vicar at the time, Reverend Gresham Kirkby, was a radical Christian socialist and wanted a new church for a new London. He championed the liturgical movement to break down the barriers between priest and people and so the concrete altar is in the centre of the room with no screens or barriers and the bright nave is lit by a geometric glass ceiling.

IF YOU GO AND VISIT THE BRUTALIST BARBICAN ESTATE IN THE CITY, YOU WILL NOTICE THAT THE CONCRETE HAS A VERY ROUGH TEXTURE. THIS EFFECT WAS ADDED AFTER CONSTRUCTION AND EVERY CHUNK OF CONCRETE WAS REMOVED BY HAND, BY A WORKMAN WITH A HAND-HELD PICK HAMMER, TO EXPOSE THE GRANITE AGGREGATE BELOW.

Burning Up

What: 20 Fenchurch Street, aka the Walkie Talkie
Where: Fenchurch Street, EC3M 3BY

Skyscraper designs do not always go to plan. During construction of 20 Fenchurch Street, aka the Walkie Talkie, a man named Martin Lindsay parked his Jaguar underneath the building, and when he returned two hours later, parts of his car had melted. The concave design of the Walkie Talkie had reflected the sun's rays down into the streets below. A 'sunshade' had to be fitted to ensure this would not happen again before it opened in 2014. The press dubbed it the 'walkie-scorchie' and the 'fry-scraper'.

The Leaning Tower of London

*What: The Leadenhall Building,
aka the Cheesegrater*
Where: Leadenhall Street, EC3V 4AB

Some of the most iconic and recognisable buildings in modern-day London are skyscrapers: for example, the Gherkin, the Shard and the Scalpel.

The Leadenhall Building, otherwise known as the Cheesegrater, is a wedge-shaped skyscraper built in 2014, designed by Richard Rogers. The distinctive shape was to ensure that it lent away from St Paul's Cathedral and maintained the protected sightline of the cathedral from Fleet Street.

Walk I

TOWER HILL STATION TO LIVERPOOL STREET STATION
(2.3 KM/1.4 MILES)

A meander through the City and its 2,000 year history, predominantly focused on architecture through the ages.

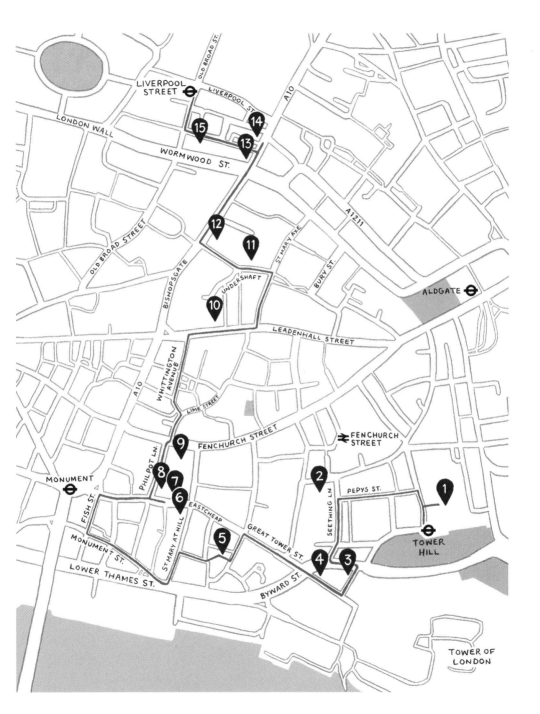

II. CRACKING THE CAPITAL'S CODE

London has an exceptionally rich and layered history. The city has had its traumas, such as the Great Fire and the Blitz, but did not undergo the wholesale remodelling that some of its European counterparts saw in the 19th century.

Therefore, the etchings and markings of each period remain – woven into the urban fabric. Symbols and emblems are passed down through the generations, their meanings sometimes obscured by time. Getting to grips with these symbols is the key to cracking the capital's code and opening the window to its fascinating past.

What's in a Name?

A Medieval Market

What: *Cheapside*
Where: *City of London, EC2V*

Many street names, particularly in the City of London – the oldest part of the metropolis – relate to a trade that once operated from there. Wood Street, Milk Street, Bread Street and Trump Street (relating to the sale of trumpets) are all examples of this.

Many of these branch off from Cheapside: one of medieval London's main market thoroughfares. The name comes from the old English word 'chepe' or *ceapan* for 'market' or 'to buy'.

Oh That's Offal

What: *Pudding Lane*
Where: *City of London, EC3R*

Other food- or trade-related names are a bit trickier to decode. Pudding Lane, for example, comes from the French word for a type of blood sausage: *boudin*. Boudin was used as a general term for offal and corrupted over time, or butchered, you could say, to 'pudding'.

It is thought that the butchers of Cheapside used the lane to transport their unwanted offal to barges on the river waiting to ferry it away for disposal.

A Lost Monastery

What: *Crutched Friars*
Where: *City of London, EC3N*

Prior to the Dissolution of the Monasteries under King Henry VIII in the 16th century, churches and monasteries owned vast amounts of land in London.

The street name Crutched Friars in the City of London relates to a monastic order founded here in 1298 known as the Friars of the Holy Cross. 'Crutched' is most likely a corruption of the word 'crossed', in reference to the friars' crucifix-topped staffs. The monastery was dissolved in 1539 and the land seized by the crown. It is said that the church itself was turned into a carpenter's yard and a tennis court.

Spot the two monk statues on Friary Court: a nod to the history of the street.

Sign Language

What: *Hanging Sword Alley*
Where: *City of London, EC4Y 1NA*

Some of the most unusual street names in London – Man in Moon Passage off Regent Street, Fox and Knot Street in Farringdon or Pope's Head Alley near Bank tube station, for example – relate to a lost pub that was once there. Before door numbers became widespread in the 18th century, shops and pubs were usually known by the symbol on their hanging sign over the front entrance. These names and symbols then often became synonymous with the street.

One outlier is the case of the ominous-sounding Hanging Sword Alley near Fleet Street. The name most likely relates to a fencing school situated there around the middle of the 16th century, its sign depicting a hanging sword.

Names are not, however, static. In the 18th century, Hanging Sword Alley was known, for a time, even more ominously, as 'Blood Bowl Alley', after an infamous drinking den.

An Arrogant Aristocrat

What: *York Place (formerly Of Alley)*
Where: *By Charing Cross station, WC2*

Near Charing Cross station look out for a little alleyway off Villiers Street called York Place. As you will see from the street sign, it was formerly known as Of Alley.

Following the Dissolution of the Monasteries, much of what was once church land passed into the hands of the aristocracy and favoured courtiers. As London's built environment expanded westwards, particularly from the 17th century onwards, many streets were named after the landowner who sold or leased the land. This area was once occupied by York House, a mansion built for the Bishops of Norwich in the 13th century and acquired by George Villiers, the Duke of Buckingham, in the 1620s.

His son, also George Villiers, sold the house in 1672 to be demolished and for streets to be laid out on the site. In an egotistical move, he sold the land on one condition: that all the streets laid out on the site would be named after him. Therefore, as requested, George Street, Villiers Street, Duke Street, Of Alley and Buckingham Street were all created to make 'George Villiers Duke of Buckingham'.

The World's Oldest Profession

What: *Cock Lane*
Where: *City of London, EC1A*

Cock Lane's name could relate to chicken breeding or cockfighting, but it is thought to most likely come from a rather different profession, some would say the world's oldest. In the medieval period, this area was one of the few places in London where brothels could operate without worrying about falling foul of the law.

In 1762 a supposed 'haunting' on the street enraptured the London public. A man called William Kent lived on Cock Lane with a lady named Fanny Lynes. Fanny died and, not long afterwards, scratching noises were heard in their lodging room. It was thought to be Fanny's ghost, returned to haunt William for supposedly murdering her. Her strange method of communication gave her the nickname 'Scratching Fanny of Cock Lane'. The noises turned out in the end to be the landlord's daughter with a concealed piece of wood.

A Forgotten Gateway

What: Bishopsgate
Where: 115 Bishopsgate, EC2M 3UE

The London Wall was first constructed by the Romans in around AD 200. Many street names in the City of London reference their location in relation to the wall, for example, London Wall, Crosswall and Houndsditch (thought to be because this was the section of perimeter ditch where Londoners tossed the remains of their dead dogs).

London's wall had six original gates, with Moorgate added in 1415 to make seven. The streets that once passed through these gates are named after them, for example Aldgate High Street. 'Ald' is thought to come

from *aeld*, meaning 'old' or potentially from 'all', as in, it was for all to pass through.

The gates were demolished in the 18th century to ease traffic, but look out for a reminder of the lost Bishopsgate on the side of 115 Bishopsgate: a modern sculpture of a bishop's mitre. It is thought the gate got its name from Erkenwald, the 7th-century Bishop of London.

A Buried River

What: Turnagain Lane
Where: City of London, EC4A

Some street names give clues to a lost London landscape, and a few reflect the location of, now buried, rivers and streams.

The Fleet, the Walbrook, the Effra and the Westbourne, among others, once flowed through the area we now think of as London but have long since been built over and subsumed into the system of drains below our feet. (See pp.151–52 for more on London's lost rivers.)

Off Farringdon Street you will find Turnagain Lane, whose name gives us a clue to the location of the lost River Fleet, which runs underneath Farringdon. The river is occasionally heard and generally unseen, but if you were to walk down Turnagain Lane prior to the 18th century, you would have come face to face with the river. You would therefore have had to ' turn again' and find another route.

Right up My Street

What: *Little Britain*
Where: *City of London, EC1A*

There are a few 'Littles' and 'Pettys' in London's panoply of street names, for example 'Petty France' and 'Petty Wales'. These relate to an immigrant community that once resided there. But how does that explain the street name Little Britain near Smithfield?

No, it doesn't relate to a certain early 2000s TV comedy series; it is thought to come from the fact that, in the early 15th century, the Duke of Brittany lived in a house here: a region of France sometimes referred to as Little Britain.

Dancing with the Devil

What: *Bleeding Heart Yard*
Where: *Holborn, EC1N*

Occasionally London street names come with layers of urban myth and legend to untangle.

The first theory behind the name Bleeding Heart Yard is that it came from an inn of the same name that was located on this site in the 16th century. It is said to have had a sign outside depicting the Virgin Mary's heart being pierced by five swords.

Another story is rather more mythical and gruesome. It involves the murder of Lady Elizabeth Hatton here on the night of 26th January 1626.

The story starts at the famous Hatton ball. The ball was in full swing when a mysterious stranger with a hunched shoulder and clawed right hand walked in. He invited Lady Hatton to dance and they proceeded to cavort and caper all night. As the ball drew to a close, they disappeared off together into the dark city. The next morning her dead body was found in the courtyard of what we now call Bleeding Heart Yard. Her heart was said to be still pumping blood over the cobbles. It was surmised that this man must have been the devil himself.

Freedom to Bear Arms

What: Bear Gardens
Where: Southwark, SE1

Street names sometimes give clues to activities long since consigned to the history books. Cockpit Steps in Westminster, for example, relates to the Royal Cockpit, a cock-fighting arena, that was once there.

Bankside, being outside jurisdiction of the City of London, was where you could attend all sorts of otherwise illicit venues such as brothels, theatres and bear-baiting pits. It was one such bear-baiting pit that gave us the street name Bear Gardens.

Bear-baiting usually involved a bear being chained up and pitted against a pack of trained baiting dogs, although other animals were also sometimes involved, including bulls and horses. Samuel Pepys described it as a 'rude and nasty pleasure'.

The pit was located on the site of Bear Gardens from at least the 16th century and the last recorded event there was the baiting of a 'fine but vicious' horse in 1682.

Stag Dos and Don'ts

What: The White Hart
Where: Great Suffolk Street, SE1 0UG; Drury Lane, WC2B 5QD; Whitechapel High Street, E1 7RA

A popular pub name across the country is The White Hart. In London you'll find a White Hart in Southwark, on Drury Lane in Covent Garden and on Whitechapel High Street, to name just three.

In 1393, during the reign of King Richard II, an act was passed to legislate that all drinking establishments must identify themselves with a sign. Richard II's personal emblem was a symbol of a white hart, or stag. Naturally then, this became a popular pub name with those trying to associate themselves with the monarch.

Other popular names relating to royal emblems include the Red Lion, a reference to the three lions on the royal coat of arms, and the Rose and Crown, thought to commemorate the end of the Wars of the Roses, when King Henry VII united the white and red roses of the houses of York and Lancaster under one crown.

Roman Roots

What: *The Holly Bush*
Where: *Hampstead, NW3 6SG*

Pub names can be a great window into the past. In Hampstead you will find a quaint little pub called The Holly Bush. The building was constructed as a stable building in 1790 and converted into a pub in 1928.

The name itself has ancient origins. When the Romans invaded Britain, they brought with them the word *taberna*, meaning a shop or stall, which might sometimes offer food and drink. It is thought this is where we get the word 'tavern' from. Tabernae would distinguish themselves with a bunch of vine leaves hanging over the front door to show that they sold wine. Without many vine leaves to hand in Britain, other small bushes were used, such as holly. The tradition, and therefore pub name, The Bush or Holly Bush were passed down through the centuries.

THERE ARE LOTS OF OTHER WORDS THAT DERIVE FROM THE LATIN BROUGHT OVER BY THE ROMANS, INCLUDING 'PLUMBING'. THE ROMANS USED LEAD IN PIPING, WHICH THEY CALLED *PLUMBUM* AND IS THE REASON ITS SYMBOL ON THE PERIODIC TABLE IS 'PB'.

Get off Your High Horse

What: *Coach and Horses*
Where: *Bruton Street, W1J 6PT;*
Hill Street, W1J 5LD

There are currently six Coach and Horses pubs in central London. For example, there is a beautiful mock-Tudor pub on Bruton Street in Mayfair, rebuilt in 1933, and another just down the road on Hill Street.

They are generally old coaching inns, or at least on the site of one. Before the railways arrived in the mid-19th century, the quickest way of getting around, if you could afford it, was by horse and carriage.

Coaching inns were particularly found in the outskirts of the city, which is why you find many in Mayfair: the edge of London in the 18th century when this mode of transport was most prevalent. The coaching inns provided hospitality and lodging for both weary humans and their horses.

Transport Links

What: Two Chairmen
Where: Westminster, SW1H 9BP

The Two Chairmen is said by some to be Westminster's oldest pub, dating back to the mid-18th century, although the current building dates from the early 20th century.

The pub sign depicts two chairmen: the burly fellows whose profession it was to transport their customers around in sedan chairs. Sedan chairs for hire were introduced into London in the early 17th century and were a popular mode of transport for the wealthy looking to keep their shoes unmuddied.

The pub name came from the fact that two of these chairmen apparently used to frequent the pub in question to wait for customers leaving the cock-fighting arena opposite.

Sedan chairs went out of fashion in the 19th century as the city grew and other modes of transport became more appropriate.

Viking London

What: St Clement Danes
Where: Strand, WC2R 1DH

Although names can be a useful historical guide, they can sometimes create more questions than answers.

No one is certain where the word 'Danes' in St Clement Danes church on Strand comes from, but there are a couple of theories. One is that the Vikings occupied this area of London, known as Aldwych, in the 9th century and established the church. Another is that when Alfred the Great retook London at the end of the 9th century, he allowed Danes who had married English women to live in this area as long as they converted to Christianity. They are said to have taken over, or built, the church of St Clements, fittingly the patron saint of mariners. Spot the anchor crest by the entrance.

It is also thought to be the burial place of Harold Harefoot, the Danish king of England from 1035–1040, son of King Cnut. But is this where the name comes from? We may never know for sure.

The Traveller's Saint

What: Churches dedicated to St Botolph
Where: Aldgate High Street, EC3N 1AB;
Bishopsgate, EC2M 3TL;
Aldersgate Street, EC1A 4EU;
Ludgate Hill, EC4M 7DE

So much of London's history is tied up in the fabric and names of its churches. The saint a church is dedicated to can give you a clue to the history of the area. St Botolph was the patron saint of travellers, so you will often find a church dedicated to him where the city gates once stood. Travellers leaving the city could therefore pray for good fortune on their adventures.

You will find a St Botolph without Aldgate, St Botolph without Bishopsgate, and St Botolph without Aldersgate. The 'without' means that it was outside the city walls, as opposed to St Martin within Ludgate, which was just inside.

Deciphering Symbols

A City Safari

What: *Livery company symbols*
Where: *Wax Chandlers' Hall, EC2V 7AD; Cutlers' Hall, EC4M 7BR; Pewterers' Hall, EC2V 7DE*

The City of London, more than anywhere else in London, is jam-packed with mysterious symbols. A significant contributing factor to this are the many coats of arms and heraldic symbols of its more than one hundred livery companies.

The livery companies started life as trading guilds; for example, fishmongers, grocers and ironmongers, many being able to trace their origins back to the medieval period. The earliest charter still in existence was given to the Weaver's Company in 1155. Most still retain links with their original trade and today are predominantly charitable networking institutions that play a role in the unique governance of the City. Members of the companies retain voting rights for key positions within the City of London Corporation and you must be a member of one of the livery companies to become the Lord Mayor.

Each company has its own coat of arms, with a colourful array of animals and mythical creatures displayed, including unicorns (the Wax Chandlers), elephants (the Cutlers: thought to relate to the ivory once used in knife handles) and seahorses (the Pewterers). These can be seen over the entrances to the livery halls in the City. Most of the animals and symbols do not relate to the trade of the company but give the company an identity and emblem.

Spot the Leopard

What: *The Goldsmiths' Company symbol*
Where: *Churchyard of St John Zachary, EC2V 7HN*

Guarding the entrance to the Churchyard of St John Zachary, one of the City of London's many pocket parks, is a golden leopard or lion head.

The church of St John Zachary was one of the many incinerated during the Great Fire of London in 1666 but never rebuilt. The garden we have today was originally laid out on the old churchyard by firewatchers in 1941, during the Blitz.

The garden is managed and maintained by the Goldsmiths' Company, who received their royal charter in 1327 and have their livery hall opposite. The 'leopard', a term often used in heraldic terms to describe a face-on lion head, is the symbol of the

Goldsmiths' Company. As well as in the garden, you will see these leopard-lions on the coat of arms and livery hall of the company.

In 1300 Edward I passed a law requiring all gold and silver to be brought to the Goldsmiths' hall to be inspected for quality. If acceptable it was stamped with the leopard head symbol, giving us the term 'hallmarked'.

Take a Seat

What: *'Barman' Underground seat cover design*
Where: *Northern, Central, Jubilee and*
Bakerloo lines

Do not think that the symbol-spotting stops as you head underground to take the tube.

Before you deposit yourself in a seat, make sure to look at the designs of the seat covers. There are a variety of designs across the network, but one of the most common and iconic is known as 'Barman', created in 2010. It was named after Christian Barman who commissioned the first moquettes (a woven fabric) for the tube in 1936.

Look closely and you will see that it incorporates the abstract outlines of four London landmarks: the London Eye, Elizabeth Tower (most commonly referred to as Big Ben), St Paul's Cathedral and Tower Bridge.

THE OLDEST MERCERS'
MAIDEN CAN BE FOUND
ON CORBET COURT IN THE
CITY OF LONDON, DATING
BACK TO 1669.

Mysterious Maiden

What: *Mercers' Maiden*
Where: *Long Acre, WC2E 9PA;*
Frederick's Place, EC2R 8AE

When, in 1515, the livery companies were given an order of precedence based on wealth and influence, the Mercers' Company came out on top. It was originally a guild for merchants, particularly in fine fabrics, most likely established in the 12th century.

Their symbol, since at least 1425, has been the figure of a woman known as the Mercers' Maiden. The origin of the symbol is unknown, but two theories include it referring to the Virgin Mary or perhaps the sign of an inn where the Mercers once met in medieval London.

Today, the Mercers' Company is still one of the wealthiest livery companies and makes significant donations to charitable institutions. They own a vast property portfolio, particularly in the Covent Garden area around Long Acre, and mark their properties with the symbol of the Mercers' Maiden.

Keep your eyes peeled and you will see her peering imperiously at you from doorways, walls and even bollards, watching your every step.

Foraging for Pineapples

What: Pineapple symbols
Where: Christchurch Greyfriars
Garden, EC1A 7BA;
Lambeth Bridge SE1 7SG

Once you start looking, you will see
them everywhere: London is covered in
pineapples. You will find them adorning
the tops of railings, on buildings and, most
famously, on the two towers of St Paul's
Cathedral. But why?

Pineapples were first brought over to
Britain from Guadeloupe by Christopher
Columbus at the end of the 15th century.
They were a rare and exotic fruit and
one that was not cultivated in Britain
successfully for at least another 150 years.

They were, therefore, extremely expensive
to buy, the equivalent of about £5,000 in
today's money for a single pineapple.

They became symbols of wealth and
status. If you were not quite rich enough to
buy a pineapple in the 18th century, it was
not uncommon for people to hire them
to place as the centrepiece of their dinner
should they be having guests over!

As well as St Paul's Cathedral, you can also see stone pineapples at Christchurch Greyfriars, a church gutted during the Blitz and now a public garden, and on top of Sir John Soane's tomb in St Pancras Gardens. The first pineapple to be cultivated in Britain is thought to have potentially been grown in Lambeth by well-known gardener John Tradescant in the 17th century. This is a reason proffered for the presence of pineapples atop the four corner pillars of Lambeth Bridge, although others say that these are in fact pinecones: an ancient symbol of hospitality.

London's Burning

What: Fire insurance plaques
Where: 9 and 11 Roupell Street, SE1 8SP;
Goodwin's Court, WC2N 4LL;
11 Princelet Street, E1 6QH

London entrepreneurs are not ones for letting a good disaster go to waste. After the Great Fire of London in 1666, the city's shrewd businessmen spotted an opportunity: fire insurance.

Paid-up clients would affix a fire insurance plaque to the outside of their house, often displaying the company logo or emblem and their policy number. This distinguished their house for the insurance company's private firefighting team. If you did not have a plaque, hard luck!

The Sun Fire Office, for example, was established in 1710. They would issue lead plaques displaying their sun emblem and often with the customer's policy number displayed below. In 1996, the company merged with Royal Insurance and became the Royal and Sun Alliance Insurance Group (RSA). RSA is thought to be the oldest documented insurance company in the world and the largest in Britain.

By the early 19th century, practices had changed, but plaques were still sometimes given out as a marketing opportunity.

There are very few left today, so you must have your wits about you to spot them.

THE HOME OF TWININGS
216 STRAND

Royal-tea

What: Royal warrants
Where: Twinings, WC2R 1AP;
Fortnum & Mason, W1A 1ER;
Gieves & Hawkes, W1S 3JR

In a city where commerce is king, shops need to do all they can to stand out.

Royal warrants of appointment have been given out since the 15th century to businesses that supply a royal court or person. In the 18th century, these businesses started displaying their royal warrant, usually incorporating the royal coat of arms, to assure passers-by of their quality.

There are currently over 800 royal warrant holders in the country, including Twinings on Strand that received its first from Queen Victoria in 1837 when she appointed Twinings as tea suppliers to her household. It has been renewed by each monarch since and you can see the royal coat of arms over the entrance to their shop on Strand where the business was first established in 1706.

THE TWININGS LOGO IS THOUGHT TO BE THE OLDEST CONTINUOUSLY USED LOGO IN THE WORLD. IT HAS NOT CHANGED AT ALL SINCE 1787.

To Arms!

What: The Bedford coat of arms
Where: Covent Garden Market Building, WC2E 8RD

The Dissolution of the Monasteries from 1536–1541 under King Henry VIII saw one of the largest transfers in land ownership in London's history. Vast tracts of church land were confiscated and given to aristocrats and favoured courtiers. Evidence of this ownership can be seen in aristocratic coats of arms around the city.

The area of Covent Garden, for example, was once owned by Westminster Abbey, previously known as the 'convent garden'. Following its confiscation in the 16th century, it was acquired by the Russell family, the Earls of Bedford. In the early 17th century, the 4th Earl of Bedford decided to build the grand piazza-style square we have today. When the market building in the centre was constructed in 1830, the Bedford coat of arms was used as a decorative motif and can be seen over the entrances. The coat of arms has a lion in the centre and the Russell family motto: *Che sara sara*, meaning 'what will be, will be'.

The Bedford family owned the land right up until 1918 when it was sold on to other private owners, but the Bedford Estate is still the largest landowner in the Bloomsbury area.

Dragons and Daggers

What: City of London coat of arms
Where: The City of London

The City of London, the ancient heart of London and today the financial district, has its own government that predates Parliament and has autonomy over some areas of its governance.

It also has its own coat of arms, thought to have been in use since at least the 14th century. It depicts two dragons flanking a shield with the red-and-white Cross of St George. In the top left quadrant of the shield is a dagger, representing the sword of St Paul. A common myth states that the dagger symbolises the one used by the Lord Mayor of London to stab and kill Wat Tyler, a leader of the Peasants' Revolt, in 1381. However, the symbol was already in place before this date. At the bottom of the coat of arms is the City of London motto: *Domine dirige nos,* meaning 'Lord, guide us'.

The red-and-white theme is applied elsewhere; for example, various items of street furniture such as bollards and the City of London police force have red and white checked hat bands as opposed to the normal black and white.

You will not just find the coat of arms in the City itself, as the City of London Corporation also manages housing estates, parks and schools across London.

Oh Deer, Oh Deer

What: Golden hind symbols
Where: Seven Dials, WC2H

Seven Dials is today one of London's popular areas for theatres, restaurants and shops, but this was certainly not always so.
Prior to 1537 when King Henry VIII seized the land, it was predominantly fields and part of the site of a leper hospital established in the 12th century. In 1690, as London was expanding, the freehold of the land was given to MP Thomas Neale who created the radial layout of Seven Dials we have today.

The Seven Dials Trust was established in 1984 to promote enhancements to the urban environment, including improving street furniture such as signage and bollards. Lots of these display the symbol of a golden hind (a female deer) wounded by an arrow. This is the emblem of St Giles and, therefore, of the ancient parish of St Giles in the Fields church established in 1101.

St Giles, patron saint of lepers and the physically disabled, was a hermit, thought to have lived in the 7th to 8th centuries. Legend says that he lived in the forest with a deer as his only companion and that one day he was hit by a hunter's arrow intended for the deer. The wounded deer was therefore used as his symbol.

Court Summons

What: Emblems of the Inns of Court
Where: Middle Temple Lane, EC4Y 9AT

One area of London particularly festooned with mysterious imagery is Temple. From the 12th century, this enclave, to the west of the City of London, was owned by the Knights Templar. The religious crusading order built the beautiful Temple Church there in 1185.

After the abolition of the order in 1312, it became a centre for lawyers and their students. They initially formed two societies: the Inner Temple and the Middle Temple. The former was located on the consecrated ground around the church and the latter on the unconsecrated land. Today they are two of the four Inns of Court: legal associations to which every barrister in England and Wales must be a member.

Walk around the atmospheric courtyards of Temple and you will undoubtedly spot the emblems of the societies, adorning railings, gates and entranceways. The emblem of the Middle Temple is the Lamb of God or Agnus Dei. This was an ancient religious symbol used by the Knights Templar; the lamb represented Jesus, the sacrificial lamb of God.

The emblem of the Inner Temple is a Pegasus. This is thought to have either derived from another symbol of the Knights Templar or, alternatively, was designed in honour of Lord Robert Dudley, who

MIDDLE TEMPLE HALL, A RARE TUDOR SURVIVOR, BUILT IN 1573, IS WHERE THE FIRST-EVER RECORDED PERFORMANCE OF SHAKESPEARE'S *TWELFTH NIGHT* TOOK PLACE ON 2ND FEBRUARY 1602.

performed in a play at the Inner Temple in 1561 as Prince Pallaphilos, patron of the fictional Order of the Pegasus.

Building Bridges

What: *The Bridge Mark*
Where: *Tower Bridge, SE1 2UP; London Bridge SE1 2PF; Blackfriars Bridge SE1 9UD; Southwark Bridge SE1 9HQ; Millennium Bridge SE1 9JE*

Tower Bridge is one of London's most recognisable icons and is crossed by thousands every day. Most, however, will miss a cryptic symbol on the two majestic towers.

It is called the Bridge Mark and is the symbol of Bridge House Estates. A charitable trust overseen by the City of London Corporation, Bridge House Estates

was set up in 1282 to maintain London Bridge, the only crossing over the Thames in central London until 1750. The Bridge Mark has been in use as the trust's symbol since the 17th century.

The profits gained from tolls and rents over the centuries were used to build Tower Bridge, Blackfriars Bridge and acquire Southwark Bridge. Most recently the trust contributed towards the construction of the Millennium Bridge.

Today, they manage all five bridges, so when crossing or admiring from the shore, keep your eyes peeled and you may well spot the Bridge Mark.

Vexing Verges

What: *Kerbstone symbols*
Where: *16–18 Whitehall, SW1A 2DY*

You will walk past hundreds if not thousands of kerb stones every day without paying them a blind bit of notice. However, take a moment to have a closer look at them and you may see that they occasionally have peculiar symbols carved into them.

There are a perplexing variety of symbols and it is safe to say that no one has yet deciphered all of them, but there are various different theories. Some are simply marks to show who the stonemason was who made it or an arrow to denote in which direction it should be placed. Other symbols are said to be 'service' marks for electricity companies, signifying a cable

joint, high voltage or a pipe below street level. At the beginning of the 20th century, London was supplied by multiple electricity companies, meaning that there was not a universal system of symbols in place.

Outside 16–18 Whitehall you will see a strange symbol carved into the kerb stones that looks like a three-pronged arrow. It is a 'pheon' or broad arrow symbol, the marker of the Board of Ordnance, a military department of the government established in the 16th century. They are here because this was once the site of the old Admiralty Building and, in the Elizabethan period, a law was brought in stipulating that all navy property must be marked with the symbol.

Setting a Benchmark

What: *Ordnance Survey benchmarks*
Where: *St Alban's Tower, EC2V 7AF;*
St Mary le Bow, EC2V 6AU

Observant urban wanderers may spot a symbol, usually carved into the sides of buildings or on a small plaque, that looks like an arrow pointing up towards a flat line.

These are Ordnance Survey benchmarks and can be used to determine height above sea level. If you know the height of one mark, then you will be able to determine the height above sea level of another by measuring the difference between them.

The last benchmark was made in 1993 with satellites taking over in the determination of height above sea level. There are still around 18,000 Ordnance Survey benchmarks to be found in Greater London, most often found carved into buildings surveyors thought would be around for a long time, for example church towers.

Entwined Royals

What: *Westminster Bridge lamp symbols*
Where: *Westminster Bridge, SE1 7GA*

Westminster Bridge is most often seen thronged with tourists taking pictures of the Houses of Parliament or the London Eye.

Take a moment, however, to admire the beautiful, Gothic Revival, triple-standard lamps along the balustrade. They were designed by Sir Charles Barry who

designed, along with Augustus Pugin, the Houses of Parliament.

In the centre of the lamps you will notice, picked out in gold, an entwined V and A. They represent the initials of Queen Victoria and her husband Prince Albert. The bridge connects the Victoria and Albert embankments and opened to vehicle traffic on the 24th May 1862, Queen Victoria's 43rd birthday and just a few months after Albert's death.

A Love Affair Hiding in Plain Sight?

What: *Westminster lamppost symbols*
Where: *City of Westminster*

When symbol spotting in the City of Westminster, make sure you look closely at the black lampposts. On one side you will see a florid, gold-coloured 'W' for Westminster and on the other side are two interlocked C-shapes that seem to resemble the Chanel logo.

In the 1920s, the 2nd Duke of Westminster, Britain's richest man at the time, had a 10-year-long affair with fashion designer Coco Chanel. The story goes that the symbol on the lampposts are some sort of romantic gesture.

The real explanation is, however, sadly far more boring. The interlocking C-shapes stand for City Council, which, when paired with the 'W', stands for Westminster City Council.

Tracking Down Trunks

What: Elephant symbols
Where: Elephant's Head, NW1 8QR;
Elephant House, NW1 8NL

Did you know Camden has a surprising link to elephants? Allow me to explain.

Camden Town was established in the late 1700s by Sir Charles Pratt, the 1st Earl of Camden. When a new coat of arms for the family was created, it incorporated the symbol of an elephant and castle, a popular heraldic emblem symbolising strength. So, when the borough of Camden was created in 1965, it incorporated the elephant symbol into its coat of arms.

On Camden High Street you will find the Elephant's Head pub, established in 1869. The name is thought to come from the Pratt family coat of arms. The link however does not stop there.

On Kentish Town Road, you will find the Elephant House. The red brick Grade II listed building opened in 1901 and was once the bottle store for the Camden Brewery. The company operated in Camden from 1859–1926 and the elephant head became their trademark after one of their most popular products called Elephant Pale Ale. As you approach the building, you will notice a terracotta elephant head decoration over the main doorway and that each of the black railings is topped by a little elephant head.

Deciphering Death

What: Gravestone symbols
Where: Highgate Cemetery, N6 6PJ;
Tower Hamlets Cemetery Park, E3 4PX;
West Norwood Cemetery, SE27 9JU

Gravestones can often be beautiful works of art and, particularly in the Victorian cemeteries, you will see a vast array of symbols and designs. Here are some of the most common:

- Anchors can often be found on the graves of seafarers but are also a symbol of steadfastness and hope.
- Clasped hands represent reunification in the afterlife.
- A square and compasses are a masonic symbol but are also occasionally seen on the graves of architects.
- A severed bud or flower usually signifies the death of a young person or child.
- Wheat is the symbol of someone who lived to a ripe old age.
- A serpent is an ancient Egyptian symbol of life, sometimes depicted biting its own tail to represent eternal life.

A 'Nazi' Dog Grave

What: The grave of Giro
Where: 9 Carlton House Terrace, SW1Y 5AG

In St James's you will find a very curious little oddity: the grave of, what has been described as, a 'Nazi' dog.

The diminutive grave marker can be found next to 9 Carlton House Terrace and pays tribute to Giro, who died in February 1934. He was the dog of Leopold von Hoesch, the German ambassador to the UK from 1932–1936, and 9 Carlton House Terrace was acting as the German embassy at this time.

When von Hoesch came over to Britain in 1932 he brought with him Giro, his pet terrier (or potentially German Shepherd). The common story is that Giro died from electrocution, having clamped his jaws around a cable in the back garden.

In 1932 von Hoesch was the ambassador for the Weimar Republic, but after Hitler seized power in 1933, he became, not by choice, the ambassador for the Nazi regime. He was, in fact, a highly respected statesman and critical of Nazi aggression and many in Hitler's inner circle.

After von Hoesch died in 1936, he was honoured with a large funeral cortege from London to Dover. No one from the Nazi party attended his funeral in Berlin. The term 'Nazi' for him and Giro, therefore, is decidedly unfair.

'Remember You Must Die'

What: Memento mori symbols
Where: Hart Street, EC3R 7NA;
Deptford Green, SE8 3DQ;
Bunhill Fields, EC1Y 2BG;
St Anne's Limehouse, E14 7HA

One of the most intriguing and morbid gravestone symbols is called a 'memento mori', Latin for 'remember you must die'. It is usually represented with a skull and crossbones but can sometimes be accompanied, or replaced, by an hourglass or coffin.

Another form of memento mori are skulls over the entrances to graveyards or on gateposts, such as at St Olave's Church Hart Street or St Nicholas Church in Deptford.

In medieval Europe the idea of memento mori was used to encourage the God-fearing populace to put off earthly pleasures and focus on making sure they had a favourable afterlife. Popularity for memento mori declined in the 17th century but had a resurgence in the Victorian period when mortality rates were high, particularly in cities, and morality became an obsession. Other good places to find memento mori symbols include Bunhill Fields Burial Ground and St George in the East church.

Home Is Where the Art Is

ALL THINGS ARTY FROM SCULPTURES TO FRIEZES AND DECORATIVE PLAQUES

A Can-destine Operation

What: Bansky artworks
Where: Bruton Lane, W1;
Chiswell Street, EC1; Tooley Street, SE1;
Stoke Newington Church Street, N16

London, like any modern city, is tagged and labelled with graffiti, much of it vandalism, but some of it absolutely fantastic street art. There are many prolific street artists in the capital but the most famous is, of course, Banksy. The anonymous artist has produced a huge amount of street art over the years in London and elsewhere. Many works have been painted over, vandalised or removed, but there are a fair few that remain. Here are some of the best preserved:

- *Shop Till You Drop*: Bruton Lane, Mayfair, W1
- *I Love Robbo Rat*: Chiswell Street, Islington, EC1
- *Rat*: Tooley Street, SE1
- *The Royal Family*: Stoke Newington Church Street, N16

London's Longest Graffiti Wall

What: The Leake Street tunnel
Where: Leake Street, SE1 7NN

Tucked away underneath the teeming Waterloo station is another hive of activity. Leake Street is the road tunnel running beneath the station and is home to London's longest legal graffiti wall, showcasing the work of some of the city's most talented street artists.

In 2008 Banksy hosted The Cans Festival in the tunnel and invited the cream of the crop of the world's street artists to create works there. From then on, its future has been sealed as one of London's best street art destinations. This explosion of colour and artistic expression is constantly evolving and changing, so every visit will be a different experience.

London's Underground Art Scene

What: *Charing Cross mural*
Where: *Northern line platform of Charing Cross*

Underground stations are not commonly thought of as creative destinations, but you will be surprised by how much art you will find on London's tube network. One example that specifically relates to the history of the area is the artwork on the Northern line platforms of Charing Cross.

A black-and-white mural depicts the construction of the medieval monument or 'cross' that gave the area its name. In 1290, Eleanor of Castile, queen to King Edward I, died near Lincoln. As her body was brought back to London, it stopped at various points and, as a romantic gesture, King Edward constructed an elaborate monument at each point. They were known as Eleanor Crosses and the final one was at the village of Charing. (The name 'Charing' comes from

the old English word *cierring*, meaning 'bend', due to its location at the curve in the River Thames.)

Look out for the Victorian replica of the Charing Cross outside Charing Cross station.

The Saint of Cheapside

What: *Thomas Becket plaque*
Where: *Cheapside, EC2V 6EB*

At the junction of Cheapside and Ironmonger Lane, look up to see a plaque affixed to the corner of number 90. It depicts Thomas of London, better known as Thomas Becket and later, Thomas à Becket.

Thomas was born here in 1120 to Gilbert, a prosperous mercer, and his wife Matilda. Thomas would go on to become Archbishop of Canterbury under King Henry II from 1162–1170 and a close friend and advisor to the King. Their relationship soured when their ideologies started to diverge over the powers of king and church. Becket was murdered by four of the King's knights in Canterbury Cathedral on the 29th of December 1170 after the King supposedly said, 'Will no-one rid me of this turbulent priest?'

Soon after his death, Thomas was canonised by Pope Alexander III and his shrine in Canterbury Cathedral became a highly important pilgrimage destination.

The Boar of the Bard

What: A boar-head sculpture
Where: 33–35 Eastcheap, EC3M 1DT

In the City of London, 33–35 Eastcheap certainly sticks out from the crowd. It's a rather bizarre neo-Gothic office block, built in 1868, that becomes even stranger when you learn that it was originally constructed as a vinegar warehouse. In the centre of the elaborate facade you will see a sculpture depicting a boar's head.

This odd architectural detail is a reference to one of London's lost pubs: the Boar's Head Inn. There had been a pub called the Boar's Head there since at least the 14th century. In the 16th century

it counted none other than William Shakespeare and his contemporaries among its patrons. Among other plays, the very same Boar's Head Inn is mentioned in Shakespeare's *Henry IV, Part 1*, as the meeting place of Sir John Falstaff and Prince Hal.

The inn was destroyed in the Great Fire of London in 1666 but rebuilt and finally demolished in 1831.

Having a Nose About

What: The Seven Noses of Soho
Where: Admiralty Arch SW1; Endell Street WC2; Windmill Street, Meard Street, D'Arblay Street, Bateman Street, Dean Street, W1

In 1997 something very odd happened in central London: roughly 35 sculpted noses appeared overnight on various buildings. Who put them there and why was a mystery for years and all sorts of urban myths grew up around them.

A nose anchored to the inside of Admiralty Arch sparked a few interesting theories. One stated that it was a spare nose for the statue of Admiral Nelson atop Nelson's Column. Another was that it was created to poke fun at Napoleon and that cavalry troops would tweak it when riding past on their horses.

It was only in 2011 that the cat was let out of the bag, by which point there were only about 10 remaining. An artist by the name of Rick Buckley revealed that he had

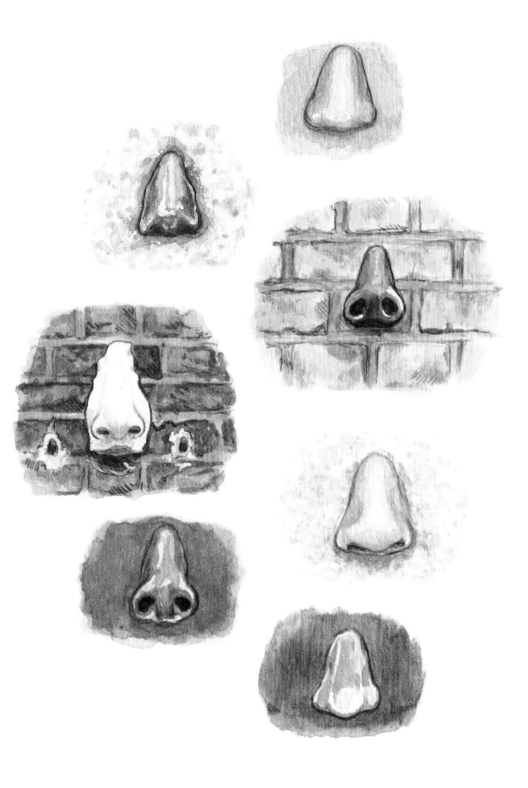

put them up as a commentary on CCTV and snooping. He also said that he simply wanted to see whether he could get away with it!

There are just seven left today and they are known as the Seven Noses of Soho, although there are thought to be a couple of fakes in there. Legend has it that, should you find them all, you will receive infinite wealth. Visit the locations listed above and have a hunt for them – good luck!

The Giants of Fleet Street

What: *Statues of Gog and Magog*
Where: *St Dunstan in the West, EC4A 2HR*

On Fleet Street in the heart of London, you will find the historic St Dunstan in the West church. Dedicated to St Dunstan, a bishop of London and Archbishop of Canterbury in the 10th century, there has been a church on this site since at least AD 1070. The church narrowly survived the Great Fire of London in 1666 but was rebuilt in 1831.

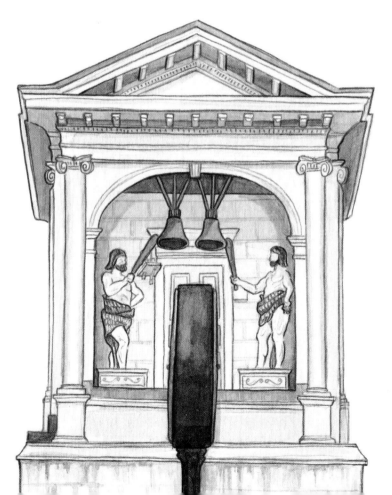

A brilliant and rather flamboyant survivor from the old church can be seen on the outside. Commissioned in 1671, you will see a beautiful clock: the first public clock in London to have a minute hand. You will also see two figures, either side of a bell, perhaps representing the giants Gog and Magog: mythical guardians of London. The two golden-loincloth-garbed muscular figures hold clubs and strike the hours and quarters between them.

While you're here, also look out for one of London's oldest statues (see p.99).

Back to School Blues

What: *Bluecoat school statues*
Where: *Caxton Street, SW1H 0PY;*
St John of Wapping, E1W 2UP

Occasionally on the front of a building you may see sculptures depicting children in blue uniforms.

These were displayed on the front of a building to denote that it was a 'bluecoat' school. These were charitable schools set up for children from deprived backgrounds. Established in 1552, Christ's Hospital in the City of London was the first. The children wore blue coats with belts, knee breeches and yellow socks. Blue was used as it was one of the cheapest dyes to obtain at the time. The socks were said to have been dyed yellow with saffron and onion to deter the rats from biting the children's ankles! Christ's Hospital moved to Horsham in Sussex in 1902, where it remains to this day.

Other charitable schools then followed with similar uniforms, and the general term 'bluecoat schools' stuck. They were replaced in the 19th century with the Victorian equivalent known as 'ragged schools', the name coming from the poor state of the children's clothing.

Old bluecoat schools, with their statues, can be found on Caxton Street and at St John of Wapping church.

Frieze, Punk!

What: A decorative frieze
Where: 135 Shaftesbury Avenue, WC2H 8AH

The decoration on a building can often give clues to its history.

A great example is the large frieze on the cinema at 135 Shaftesbury Avenue in Covent Garden. The building opened in 1931, designed by TP Bennett & Son, as the Saville Theatre. It was used as a theatre until 1965 when it was leased by the Beatles' manager, Brian Epstein, and presented both plays and rock-and-roll shows.

In 1970 it was converted into a cinema, but the frieze, designed by Gilbert Bayes, around the outside of the building,

points to its theatrical past. It is called *Drama Through the Ages* and depicts various scenes from theatrical productions and styles throughout history, including Roman gladiators, a group of travelling minstrels and scenes from Shakespeare's plays.

A Mysterious Carving

What: The Panyer Boy
Where: Panyer Alley, EC1M 8AD

On Panyer Alley next to St Paul's Cathedral, you will find a curious stone carving of a figure affectionately known as the Panyer Boy. No one knows for sure where it came

from, what building it originally adorned or exactly what it depicts.

The boy is depicted sitting on a mysterious object – perhaps a breadbasket, a coil of rope, a fruit basket or a sack. Below is the inscription: 'When ye have sought the Citty Round. Yet still this is the highest ground. August the 27, 1688.' It's thought that this confusing inscription relates to Panyer Alley being one of the highest points in the City. And the street might also provide clues to deciphering the rest of the plaque.

Panyer Alley is most likely so called because of the boys who used to sell bread here from baskets or 'panniers'. John Stow, writing in the 16th century, says the alley was named after a sign depicting a boy sitting on a breadbasket. Perhaps today's Panyer Boy is that sign or a later reconstruction. Others think it could be the sign for a pub called The Panyer that was located here until 1666.

The building that the Panyer Boy was on was demolished in 1892 but thankfully he was saved from the wrecking ball. He has since been moved around from wall to wall as the city has morphed and modernised around him.

The Golden Boy of Pye Corner

What: *Statue of the Golden Boy*
Where: *Giltspur Street, EC1A 9DD*

One of the best oddities in London is the Golden Boy of Pye Corner. This chubby little chap furnishes the corner of the building at the junction of Cock Lane and Giltspur Street. (See p.60 for the story behind Cock Lane).

The roughly 60-centimetre (2-feet)-high statue depicting a naked boy is made from wood and originally sported a pair of wings. He dates from the 17th century and was put up to mark the point where the Great Fire of London stopped. The plaque beneath him reads: 'This Boy is in Memmory Put up for the late FIRE of LONDON Occasion'd by the Sin of Gluttony 1666'. The sin of gluttony was one of the reasons surmised at the time as to why God was punishing the people of London and is said to be the reason the statue is 'prodigiously fat'.

London's Second St Paul's Cathedral

What: *'Architecture' bronze*
Where: *Vauxhall Bridge, SW8 2JW*

Did you know London has two St Paul's Cathedrals?

Not that you'd know from walking across it, but from the shore you can see that Vauxhall Bridge is home to eight huge bronze symbolic figures.

The current Vauxhall Bridge opened in 1906 but was considered too bland. In 1907 the statues, designed by Alfred Drury and F.W. Pomeroy, were added, representing Education, Local Government, Fine Arts, Science, Pottery, Engineering, Architecture and Agriculture.

Roughly halfway along on the upstream side, lean (carefully) over the edge to see a miniature St Paul's Cathedral, held lovingly in the arms of the Architecture sculpture.

Oh Dam

What: *A beaver weathervane*
Where: *60–62 Bishopsgate, EC2N 4AW;*
105–109 Oxford Street, W1D 2HQ

On bustling Bishopsgate, now dwarfed by colossal skyscrapers, you will see a building topped with an attractive cupola, finished with a shining golden weathervane. If you look closely, you will see that it is in the form of a beaver.

The beaver is the emblem of the Hudson's Bay Company, based here at 60–62 Bishopsgate from 1926. The company was established in 1670 to occupy the land by Hudson's Bay in modern-day Canada and carry out commercial activities. They made vast profits, particularly by trading fur, most notably beaver pelts.

For more beavers, go to 105–109 Oxford Street and look up at the roof. You will see a team of three beaver sculptures peering down at you. If you go around the back of the building, all will become clear, and you will see a ghost sign telling you that this building was once the home of Henry Heath's Hat Factory. Their main product was top hats made from felted fur. The most sought-after fur? Beaver, for its waterproof qualities.

Got the Hump

What: *The camels of Eastcheap*
Where: *20 Eastcheap, EC3M 1EB*

Walk along Eastcheap and you will come across a rather unusual sight: three camels being led across a desert.

No, it is not some sort of mirage but the frieze above number 20, known as Peek House. The building was constructed in the 1880s as the headquarters of the Peek Brothers & Co: importers of tea, coffee and spices. At the height of their success, they accounted for five per cent of the tea trade into London.

The camels were carved by William Theed the Younger and were the company's trademark. The three camels are said to represent their main trades in tea, coffee and spices and, for a time, they traded their tea under the 'Camel' brand name.

The Devil's in the Detail

What: *The Cornhill Devils*
Where: *54–55 Cornhill, EC3V 3PD*

As you pass 54–55 Cornhill, look up to the roof to see three ferocious-looking gargoyles, or to be more precise, 'grotesques' (gargoyles should have some sort of waterspout or deflection incorporated).

The story goes that when this building was designed in 1893, it encroached on the land of St Peter's Cornhill church next door.

The rector kicked up a big fuss and the plans had to be changed, no doubt causing the architect Ernest Augustus Runtz a bit of a headache. It is said that Ernest had these menacing grotesques added to stare down at the rector as he arrived or left work each day. One of the grotesque's faces is even said to have been modelled on the rector.

Mutilation on Strand

What: *'Ages of Man' sculptures*
Where: *Zimbabwe House, WC2R 0JR*

At 429 Strand is Zimbabwe House. It was built in 1908 and designed by Charles Holden as the headquarters of the British Medical Association. Around the outside there are a series of 18 sculptures by Sir Jacob Epstein called the 'Ages of Man', depicting the cycle of human life from birth to death, but the modern viewers will find them somewhat deformed.

When the sculptures were erected, they caused a bit of a stir in Edwardian society. The press were in uproar and the police were even called out to inspect them. It was apparently thought that they could 'corrupt the minds of the young'.

However, that is not why today the statues appear to be mutilated. In the 1930s the sculptures started to be corroded by acid rain. One day the head of one of the figures fell onto the foot of a passer-by and it was therefore decided that all extraneous limbs and appendages needed to be lopped off.

London's Smallest Sculpture

What: 'Two Mice Eating Cheese' sculpture
Where: Philpot Lane, EC3M 1DE

Blink and you'll miss it. On Philpot Lane, you will find a tiny sculpture; in fact, it is said to be London's smallest public sculpture.

It depicts two mice fighting over a piece of cheese. The story goes that a construction worker working at height on a nearby building noticed that some of his sandwiches had been eaten. He accused a fellow worker of having taken a cheeky nibble when he wasn't looking, and a fight ensued. Both workers fell to their deaths from the building, only for it to be discovered that it was, in fact, mice that had eaten the sandwich.

The sculpture is said to commemorate the two men and the incident. As with any urban myth like this, who knows how much truth there is to it, but perhaps there is a grain in there somewhere.

THE UK'S LARGEST SCULPTURE IS SAID TO BE THE ARCELORMITTAL ORBIT IN THE QUEEN ELIZABETH OLYMPIC PARK IN STRATFORD. IT IS 114.5 METRES (376 FEET) HIGH.

Ship Ahoy!

What: *The Lloyd's Register building decoration*
Where: *71 Fenchurch Street, EC3M 4BS*

At 71 Fenchurch Street you will find the Collcutt Building, constructed from 1899–1901 and designed by Thomas Edward Collcutt.

The facade is decorated with sculpted details by Sir George Frampton depicting allegories of trade and references to shipping. On the corner are two bronze ladies, both holding little model ships to personify 'steam' and 'sail'. You will also notice a gorgeous gold weathervane in the shape of a ship.

The reason for all these maritime references is that the building was constructed as the headquarters of Lloyd's Register. Lloyd's Register began life in Edward Lloyd's coffee house in the City, popular among shipowners and ship underwriters. In 1760 customers of the coffee house banded together to form the Register Society to provide information on the quality of shipping and equipment. Lloyd's Register is still going today, providing maritime expertise across the world.

Ancient Egypt in London

What: *Cleopatra's Needle*
Where: *Victoria Embankment, WC2N 6PB*

The oldest man-made object on the streets of London is thought to be Cleopatra's Needle. This ancient Egyptian obelisk was first erected in Egypt in around 1450 BC for the Pharaoh Thutmose III in the city of Heliopolis, making it nearly 3,500 years old. It was given to Britain in 1819 by the ruler of Egypt at the time to pay thanks for the British victories over Napoleon at the Battle of the Nile and of Alexandria in 1798 and 1801 respectively.

It was only in 1877 that the British actually raised the funds to transport it to Britain and the journey was anything but smooth sailing. A vessel, that looked like a huge iron cylinder, was specifically designed to hold the 200-tonne giant and be pulled behind a ship. At one point it was cut off and floated, lost, in the Bay of Biscay for five days before being found again. Sadly six crew members' lives were lost trying to recover it and they are commemorated on a plaque at the base of the Needle.

Two sphinxes were added either side when it was erected on the embankment but are said to be facing the wrong way: they should be facing outwards to guard the Needle, not inwards. Also, make sure you spot the shrapnel damage from a World War One bomb on the base of the right-hand sphinx (see p.51).

Set in Their Ways

LONDON'S MOST UNUSUAL STATUES

Where Is the Oldest Statue in London?

What: Alfred the Great statue and Elizabeth I statue
Where: Trinity Church Square, SE1 4HT;
St Dunstan in the West, EC4A 2HR

There are two main contenders for the title of London's oldest statue.

In the blue corner, we have Alfred the Great in Trinity Church Square. It has long been thought that this statue could be medieval. However, conservation work in 2021 revealed that, in fact, the top half is 18th century, made from Coade stone, only produced from the 1770s onwards. The bottom half, however, is made of Bath stone, and thought by academics to be Roman, dating from the 2nd century. It is said to have once been the bottom half of a 3-metre (10-feet)-tall Roman statue of the goddess Minerva.

In the red corner is the statue of Elizabeth I on the side of St Dunstan in the West church on Fleet Street. This has '1586' carved into the base and once adorned the front of the Ludgate into the City of London before it was demolished in 1760. It is the only statue of Elizabeth I on the streets of London and the only surviving one carved in her lifetime, so a real historical treasure.

The Missing Statue

What: Cavendish Square's empty plinth
Where: Cavendish Square, W1G 0PR

You may well have heard of the Fourth Plinth in Trafalgar Square, which for 150 years was left empty but now hosts art installations that change every couple of years. But did you know London has another empty plinth?

At the centre of Cavendish Square in Marylebone, there once stood a statue of Prince William, Duke of Cumberland, erected in 1770. The Duke of Cumberland had won a decisive victory over the Jacobites at Culloden in Scotland in 1746 and the statue was raised in his honour by a friend. It was apparently deliberately positioned pointing north towards Scotland.

His popularity did not last, however, as it transpired that he had been ruthlessly brutal in his suppression of the Scots, ordering that no mercy be given. Following the battle, Highlanders and their culture were mercilessly crushed, and when Londoners heard of the atrocities, they were outraged. When the statue had to be taken down in 1868 to be recast, it was never put back up.

In 2012, a Korean artist, Meekyoung Shin, recreated the statue out of soap, which gradually, over time, dissolved and disappeared: a statement on the shifting meanings of statues.

The Beast of the Embankment

What: The South Bank Lion
Where: Westminster Bridge, SE1 7GA

Guarding the southern end of Westminster Bridge, you will find a mighty beast: the South Bank Lion. This magnificent statue, made from Coade stone (see p.32), was created in 1837 for the Lion Brewery, which once stood on the site of Royal Festival Hall.

The brewery was demolished in 1949 but the lion was thankfully saved. Who stepped in to save the lion? King George VI himself apparently.

London's Longest Death Stare

What: Oliver Cromwell statue and Charles I bust
Where: St Margaret Street, SW1P 3JX;
St Margaret's Church SW1P 3JX

Next to Westminster Hall, look out for the imperious statue of Oliver Cromwell. It was erected in 1899 and designed by Sir Hamo Thornycroft.

If you turn around and look to the other side of the road, you will see a bust of none other than King Charles I, his old nemesis, staring straight at him. The bust sits in a niche on St Margaret's Church and has been there since 1956 when it was donated to the church by the Society of King Charles the Martyr.

There is an urban myth that the gaze of Oliver Cromwell is averted downwards so that he is not looking directly into the eyes of Charles I, but the dates of installation prove this to be wrong.

London's Luckiest Statue

What: *Charles I statue*
Where: *Charing Cross, SW1A 2DX*

In the centre of the busy Charing Cross traffic island by Trafalgar Square is an equestrian statue of King Charles I. Commissioned in 1630, during Charles' reign, this statue is the oldest bronze statue in London.

During the English Civil War, Parliament ordered that it be removed and broken down and was taken to a metalsmith called John Rivett for the task. However, instead of destroying it, he hid it in his garden. Clearly a man with an eye for business, he did not just dupe the authorities, he also duped the public into buying knives and forks supposedly made from the metal of the statue!

He revealed the statue after the restoration of King Charles II in 1660, and in 1675, it was placed in its current location, ironically looking down Whitehall to where he was beheaded outside Banqueting House on the 30th January 1649.

THE OFFICIAL 'CENTRE' OF LONDON IS CHARING CROSS, WHERE THE STATUE OF CHARLES I STANDS.

The Cross-eyed Statue

What: *John Wilkes statue*
Where: *Fetter Lane, EC4A 1ES*

On Fetter Lane in the City of London is a statue of John Wilkes.

John Wilkes was an 18th-century popular radical MP, journalist and fighter for liberty. A champion of parliamentary reform, religious tolerance and supporter of US independence, he was expelled from Parliament twice and, at one stage, imprisoned for libel.

He lived a fascinating life and his statue on Fetter Lane was erected by admirers in 1988. The statue is true to his likeness right down to his cross-eyed countenance.

Myth-busting

What: *Various equestrian statues*
Where: *Trafalgar Square, WC2N 5DN;*
Whitehall, SW1A 2NP;
Holborn Circus, EC1N 8AA

You may have heard the common urban myth that by looking at the horse's legs on an equestrian statue, you can determine how the person died.

Two hooves off the ground supposedly signifies death in battle, one hoof that they were injured in battle and/or died of the wounds and all four hooves firmly on the ground meaning that they died due to non-military causes.

The theory is, in fact, poppycock, but a surprising proportion do follow the rules. There are many equestrian statues in London, most of which support the theory. For example, the statue of the corpulent King George IV's horse on Trafalgar Square, has all four hooves on the ground and he died from the rupture of a blood vessel in his stomach. Six of them, however, do not; for example, the statue of Earl Haig on Whitehall shows one hoof up, but he died of a heart attack. The statue of Prince Albert on Holborn Circus has one hoof raised, but he certainly did not get anywhere near a battlefield; he died in 1861, from, what was diagnosed at the time, typhoid fever.

So, next time a know-it-all tries to tout this urban myth, you can respectfully prove them wrong.

THE EQUESTRIAN STATUE OF THE DUKE OF WELLINGTON BY BANK STATION DATES FROM 1844. IT IS MADE FROM METAL FROM MELTED-DOWN CANNONS CAPTURED AT THE BATTLE OF WATERLOO. FOR THOSE WONDERING, THE HORSE HAS ALL FOUR HOOVES ON THE GROUND, WHICH WOULD SUPPORT THE MYTH, AS THE DUKE DIED FROM A STROKE.

Mole Hills into Mountains

What: *King William III statue*
Where: *St James's Square, SW1Y 4LE*

A majestic statue of King William III, erected in 1808, stands at the centre of the lovely St James's Square.

Look closely underneath the horse's back-left hoof and you will see an unusual mound. This mound is said to represent the mole-hill that tripped up the King's horse at Hampton Court Palace in 1702, causing the King to fall to the ground. Not long afterwards, William died from pneumonia due to complications from the injuries.

Supporters of King James II, deposed by William in the Glorious Revolution of 1688, were said to raise a toast to 'the little gentleman in the velvet waistcoat'.

But is it true? Well, the mound is certainly more pronounced than on any other statue in London but whether this was intentional or simply structural is unclear. Truth or urban myth, it makes for an interesting story either way!

Walk II

A walk through the heart of London, highlighting the city's hidden symbols and mysterious artworks.

1   105–109 Oxford Street beaver sculptures (see Oh Dam, p.92)
2   Rough location of one of the seven noses of Soho on D'Arblay St (see Having a Nose About, p.86). See if you can find more along the walking route!
3   Meard Street sign (see London's Oldest Street Sign, p.110)
4   Georgian shopfront at 88 Dean Street (see Shop 'Til you Drop, p.37)
5   Soho Square hut (see A Whole Lot of Hot Air, p.129)
6   Cinema frieze at 135 Shaftesbury Avenue (see Frieze, Punk!, p.90)
7   Golden hind symbols (see Oh Deer, Oh Deer, p.76)
8   Rough location of one of the Mercers' Maidens (see Mysterious Maiden, p.70)
9   Covent Garden Underground station (see Tiles for Trains, p.44)
10 Bedford coat of arms at Covent Garden Market (see To Arms!, p.75)
11 Fire insurance plaques and gas lamps at Goodwin's Court (see London's Burning, p.73; Shedding Light ..., p.123)
12 Zimbabwe House sculptures (see Mutilation on Strand, p.94)
13 King George IV statue (see Myth-busting, p.101)
14 Police look-out post (see London's Smallest Police Station, p.138)
15 Charles I statue (see London's Luckiest Statue, p.101)

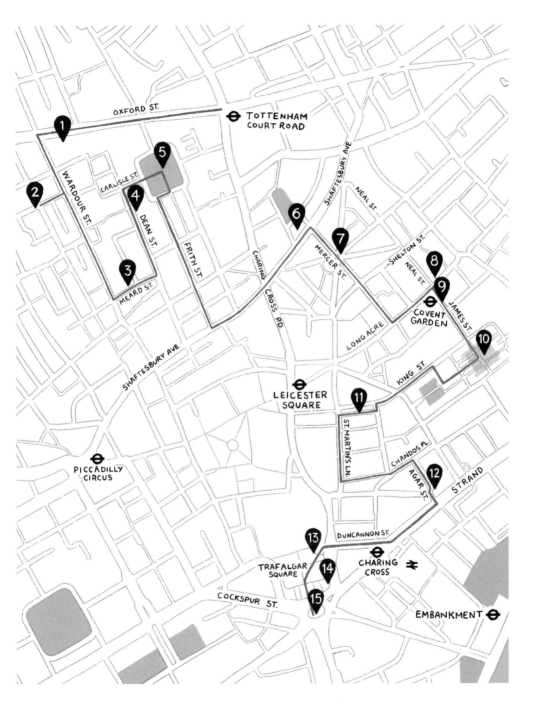

III. PART OF THE STREET FURNITURE

You'll pass by hundreds, if not thousands, of street furniture items every day as you walk around London, from lampposts to bollards, from coal-hole covers to street signs. This chapter is all about taking a moment to stop and look at these seemingly purely functional items, to appreciate the often fascinating stories behind them and to learn how they can give us illuminating glimpses into London's past.

Getting from A to B

FUNCTIONAL FURNITURE FOR FINDING YOUR WAY

London's Streets Are Paved with... Wood?

What: *Wood block paving*
Where: *259 Camden High Street, NW1 8QR; 335 Upper Street, N1 0PB; Chequer Street EC1Y 8NR*

'London's streets are paved with gold,' said Dick Whittington in the famous Victorian tale. Figuratively maybe, but, in reality, unfortunately not.

In the 18th century, stone cobbles were the most popular choice of paving; however, as the use of carriages started to increase, a problem arose: noise. Horseshoes and iron wheels on granite cobbles were incredibly loud and often slippery. Wood block paving was therefore installed along most of central London's busiest thoroughfares in the 19th century.

It was more durable, cheaper to maintain and apparently caused less accidents.

It did have some drawbacks, however; it was very hard to clean and would soak up the offending liquids a city produces, namely horse urine. The stench was said to be unbearable.

As automobiles took over from the 1920s, the wood was generally replaced with asphalt and tar, but some roads were still paved with wood right up until the 1950s.

Look out for the odd drain or manhole cover that has not been replaced and still contains wooden blocks, such as on Camden High Street and Upper Street near Angel. There is also a small section of road on Chequer Street in Islington still paved with wooden blocks.

Bollard Battles

What: *Cannon bollards*
Where: *Bankside, SE1 9HA; St Helen's Bishopsgate, EC3A 6AT*

You might not have spent much time gazing lovingly at London's bollards, but if you were to, you may well notice that many of them look rather like upended cannon barrels. That is because some of them are.

Upended cannon were used as mooring posts and bollards in the city for centuries, particularly around the dock areas, as a convenient way of repurposing old cannon. The word bollard comes from the French word *bole*, meaning a short wooden mooring post.

There is a cannon bollard in Bankside by Southwark Bridge, on which you can see the stumps left when the trunnions (the protrusions that allowed it to sit in a carriage) were removed. There is also a cannon outside St Helen's Bishopsgate in the City that is thought to be of French origin.

The oft-touted urban myth is that many bollards around London are French cannon captured at the Battle of Trafalgar, however, no French warships were ever brought back to Britain after the battle, so this is highly unlikely.

Lots of modern bollards have been designed to be in keeping with this look, complete with a rounded top to look like a cannonball.

On Your Guard

What: Guard stones
Where: Holland Park Mews, W11 3SX

At the entrance to a narrow mews or cobbled lane, look out for what is known as a 'guard stone'.

They are stone protrusions that hark back to a time of horse-drawn vehicles. As the wheels of carriages and coaches generally protruded from the body of the vehicle, they were prone to colliding with gateposts and the corners of buildings. Guard stones were therefore put in place as a kind of protective bollard.

London's Oldest Street Sign

What: Yorke Street sign
Where: 34–36 Tavistock Street, WC2E 7PB

Widespread street signage came into being after the Great Fire of London in 1666 to try to better order the city and ensure emergencies could be dealt with more easily.

London's oldest street sign, however, pre-dates the Great Fire. Dating from 1636, it is a stone tablet at the very top of a building at 34–36 Tavistock Street, displaying the street's previous name, 'Yorke Street'. The oldest street signs tend to be stone tablets with dates inscribed into them, such as on 128 the Highway in the East End (1678), Barton Street in Westminster (1722) and Meard Street in Soho (1732).

A Sign of the Times

What: Street signs
Where: Victoria Park Road, E9 7JN

There has never been an agreed uniform design for street signs, so you will see a whole variety of materials, colours and fonts around London. In Hampstead, for example, you will find some beautiful black-tiled signs with white letters or, elsewhere in the city, the occasional blue enamel plate sign.

There are a couple of clues to look out for to help date a street sign.

Numbered postcodes only came into being in 1917 during World War One. Many post office workers had gone to war, meaning that new systems were needed to help assist the replacement staff. An example can be seen on Victoria Park Road, displaying the postcode 'NE', without a number. This is a particularly interesting one because the NE district was merged into the E district ten years after its inception in 1856 due to lower post traffic. Signs were, however, still produced displaying the NE district code years afterwards because north-east London residents did not want to be seen as east-enders.

The borough displayed on a street sign can also help date it. For example, if you spot the borough of St Pancras on a street sign, then this predates 1965, when this borough was incorporated into the borough of Camden. (See more on boroughs on p.114).

End of the Road

What: Streets in the City of London
Where: The City of London

You may have heard that there are no roads in the City of London. This is very nearly true. Every thoroughfare located entirely within the City of London ends in a word that is not 'Road'. They instead end in 'Street', 'Alley', 'Place' or 'Court', for example.

The most prevalent theory on why this might be is that the layout and names of the City of London's streets were set before the use of the word 'road' for the purpose we use it for today. It is thought the word road only started to be used towards the end of the 16th century to mean an inner-city street or thoroughfare and was potentially only thought of as a long thoroughfare from one town or city to another.

However, there actually is a road within the City of London. Goswell Road runs from the Barbican up to Angel and is, therefore, half within the City and half in the borough of Islington. Half the road was incorporated into the City in 1994 when boundaries were adjusted.

THE TWO NARROWEST
ALLEYWAYS IN CENTRAL
LONDON ARE BRYDGES PLACE
BY TRAFALGAR SQUARE AND
EMERALD COURT IN BLOOMSBURY.

An Underground City?

What: Underground street signs
Where: Charing Cross Road, W1D 4TA

Step 1: Walk onto the traffic island in the middle of Charing Cross Road outside the Coach & Horses pub.
Step 2: Peer through the metal grate at your feet.
Step 3: Spot the signs visible below street level displaying the name 'Little Compton Street'.

According to some, the signs are evidence of a secret underground city: a past London lost to increasing ground levels. This, however, is not true.

What you are, in fact, looking at is a service tunnel for wires and pipes. The street signs are there so that the technicians working in the tunnel know where they are. Little Compton Street is a road that no longer exists, lost when Charing Cross Road was created in 1886.

Setting Boundaries

What: Parish boundary markers
Where: 56 Carey Street, WC 2A 2JB

In the early 19th century, before boroughs were formed, church parishes still played a key role in local decisions, including being able to raise a local tax to carry out various administrative duties. It was, therefore, very

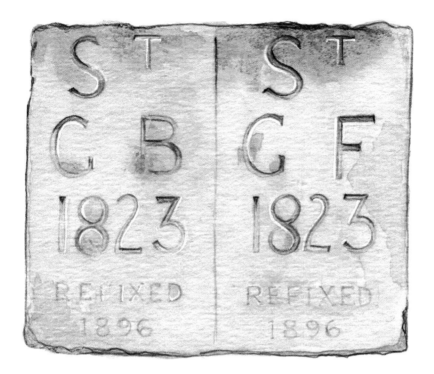

important for you to know what parish you lived in. Enter the parish boundary marker.

Parish boundary markers are often found in the form of metal or stone plaques affixed to walls or sometimes as stone blocks, dating from the 17th–19th centuries. They will tell you the, often abbreviated, name or names of the church parish boundaries it is marking.

There are two adjacent boundary markers behind the Royal Courts of Justice on Carey Street, potentially dating from the 17th century, with the letters 'WSD' on one for St Dunstan in the West on Fleet Street and an anchor symbol on the other for St Clement Danes church on Strand. It can sometimes take a bit of sleuthing to work out what they mean, particularly if they refer to churches that are long since gone.

All sound quite confusing? Well, it probably was to the people at the time too. Every year, therefore, a ceremony would take place called 'beating the bounds' in which a 'beating party' would walk around and beat the markers with sticks in an attempt to reinforce the boundaries in the minds of Londoners. Some churches continue the tradition to this day, such as All Hallows by the Tower.

Boroughly Confusing

What: *Borough names on street furniture*
Where: *All over the city*

Plastered all over London's street furniture, you will often find the name of the borough in which it sits.

In 1899 London was divided into 28 metropolitan boroughs for the purposes of local administration. In 1965 these were amalgamated into 12 inner-city boroughs, each with its own town hall, coat of arms and signature font/style. Therefore, if you see reference to the, now lost, boroughs of Finsbury, Shoreditch, Stepney, Deptford or Camberwell, for example, the sign predates 1965.

In some cases, the names of the original boroughs were simply combined to create a new one, for example, 'The Royal Borough of Kensington and Chelsea'. The 'Royal' was assigned in 1901 due its royal significance with Kensington Palace in the borough.

These inner-city boroughs were combined with 20 outer-city boroughs to create 'Greater London'.

Peculiar Pointers

What: *War department markers*
Where: *Near Tower Hill Terrace, EC3N 4EE; Artillery Lane, E1 7LJ*

Around the vicinity of the Tower of London, keep your eyes peeled for a series of intriguing markers on short iron posts displaying a broad arrow symbol, the letters 'WD' and a number, for example, 'No. 8'.

They denote the boundary of the Liberties of the Tower of London. Being a palace and garrison, the Tower and its locality had a special administrative status, managed by the War Department, hence 'WD'. The symbol was previously used by the Board of Ordnance, an early 16th century military department (see p.79). There are

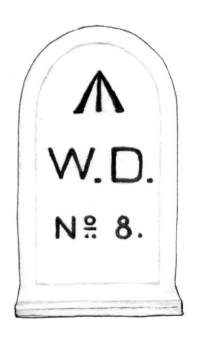

22 markers in an arc from Tower Stairs in the west to Tower Bridge in the east, laid out from 1868. There is one near the stairs to Tower Hill Terrace, for example. The Liberties were incorporated into the County of London in 1894, but the boundaries are still 'beaten' every three years by the Chapel Royal of St Peter ad Vincula in the Tower of London (see p.113 for more on 'beating the bounds').

You may also spot an occasional black arrow marker in Spitalfields, for example on the building where Artillery Passage meets Artillery Lane. These mark out an area of land that, prior to 1682, was used as an artillery ground.

Swings and Roundelbouts

What: *The London Underground roundel*
Where: *Covent Garden station, WC2E 9JT;*
Moorgate station, EC2Y 9AG; Maida Vale
station, W9 1JS

One of the city's most iconic symbols is the London Underground roundel. The first roundel with the station name displayed on it was installed at St James's Underground station in 1908: a solid red enamel circle with a horizontal blue bar. You can still see one of these original designs at Covent Garden tube station. It was also in this year that the various companies running the underground railways agreed to use 'Underground' as the general term for their services.

There were a couple of variations initially, for example in 1914 the Metropolitan line introduced its own diamond-shaped version. Examples of this design were installed at Moorgate station in 2013 to celebrate the 150th anniversary of the Metropolitan line. Another unusual roundel to look out for is the mosaic roundel at Maida Vale station, created in 1915 when the station opened.

In 1915 the new Johnston typeface was created by Edward Johnston, still used today with small changes made in the 1970s and 2016 by Eiichi Kono.

By 1919 the roundel was appearing all over the network and in 1933 the various companies running the network merged to form the London Passenger Transport Board, the forerunner for Transport for London, with the roundel as its logo.

Today a 'family' of roundels have been developed for each mode of transport, with different colours for Overground, Cycles, DLR, River Transport and Trams.

Beck in Business

What: *The Underground map*
Where: *Temple Tube station, WC2R 2PH*

The London Tube map is another London icon, but why does it look the way it does?

The original Tube map, created in 1908, was a geographically accurate representation of where the Tube lines went. But this resulted in a pretty unintelligible jumble of lines and names written at different angles, particularly in central London where stations were very close to each other.

Improvements were made over the proceeding couple of decades, but it was not until 1931 when an Underground electrical draughtsman by the name of Harry Beck, in his free time, had a go at solving the problem. He based his map on electrical circuit diagrams: neat, with straight lines, diagonals, curved angles and evenly spaced gaps between the stations. We still use that map to this day, and the method was exported to underground networks all over the world. This map was first issued as a pocket edition in January 1933. His reward for the work? Just £10 (the equivalent of £600 today).

Check the outside of Temple station for a pre-Beck vintage Tube map from 1932.

All Aboard!

What: *London's tram network*
Where: *14–16 Southampton Row, WC1B 4AP*

Introduced in 2000, South London has a small tram network linking Croydon, Beckenham and Wimbledon. London however, used to have a much more widespread network across the whole city.

The first tram line was introduced in 1860 along Victoria Street in Westminster, set up by a man ironically named George Francis Train. It was initially horse-drawn, becoming electric in 1901. Bar Westminster and the City, where wealthy landowners

and businesses kicked up a fuss, the trams ran all over the city.

The network was abolished in 1952 for 'obstructing traffic', but there is some evidence to look out for today. Look down at the pavements and you will occasionally see an old service hatch cover with the words 'London County Council Tramways'. On Southampton Row in Holborn you can see the entrance to a tram tunnel, complete with tracks, that opened in 1906 to link Holborn to the Victoria Embankment.

Finding Shelter

What: *World War Two air-raid shelter signs*
Where: *Lord North Street, SW1P 3LA; Tanner's Hill, SE8 4QB; 42 Brook Street, W1K 5DB*

Very occasionally in London you can spot the, now faded, signs pointing to

underground bomb shelters used during the Blitz. Often they are just a large black or white 'S' on a background of the alternate colour and sometimes accompanied by an arrow or explanatory words.

They were designed to stand out in the dark as blackout regulations were introduced in the UK on the 1st September 1939 and were only lifted in April 1945. As well as the white air-raid shelter signs, kerbs, trees and lampposts would be painted white to show up in the dark at ground level.

Some of the most noticeable in central London are on Lord North Street in Westminster, pointing to 'public shelters in vaults under pavements'. You will find others over the railway bridge on Tanner's Hill in Lewisham and at 42 Brook Street in Mayfair.

At Your Convenience

FUNCTIONAL FURNITURE THAT IMPROVES CITY LIFE

A Royal Letter

What: *Postbox regnal ciphers*
Where: *Fleet Street, EC4A 2BJ*

Once you start postbox hunting, no walk through the city will ever be the same again.

Following the introduction of a centralised Uniform Penny Post system, the first traditional British pillar postbox was introduced to the island of Jersey in 1852.

The rest of mainland Britain followed over the subsequent years.

The regnal cipher on the front of each postbox will tell you in which monarch's reign it was erected. Each monarch from Queen Victoria onwards has their own regnal symbol, usually combining their initial and regnal number. The most common you will see around London are, of course, Queen Elizabeth II postboxes. Queen Victoria postboxes are the oldest and come in slightly different designs such as the early Penfold postbox. You can find a Queen Victoria postbox on Fleet Street outside number 141.

You can consider yourself a postbox hunting champion if you spot an Edward VIII postbox. King Edward VIII only sat on the throne for less than a year in 1936 before abdicating to marry divorcee Wallis Simpson and so very few were erected during his reign.

It's Not That Easy Being Green

What: A green postbox
Where: St Martin's Le Grand, EC1A 4ER

On St Martin's Le Grand in the City of London, you will find an unusual green, hexagonal postbox.

It is a replica green Penfold postbox erected in 2016 to mark the 500th anniversary of the founding of the first post office under King Henry VIII.

Penfold postboxes, named after their designer John Penfold, were installed from 1866–1879. The first postboxes were erected on Jersey in 1852 and were painted red. Green then came into vogue, but from 1874 onwards, postboxes were painted red again as people had apparently been struggling to spot the green ones.

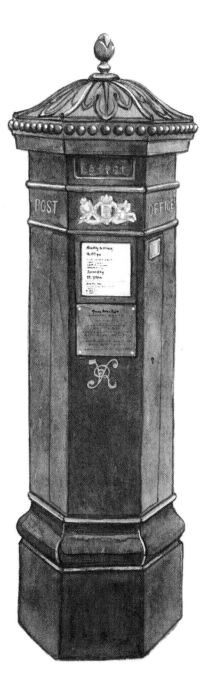

Ladies and gents

What: Ex-public toilets turned cocktail bars
Where: Ladies and Gentlemen, NW5 1NR;
Bermondsey Arts Club, SE1 4TP;
CellarDoor, WC2R 0HS

As London's population grew rapidly in the 19th century, sanitation became an increasingly pressing issue.

In 1851 an engineer called George Jennings introduced the flush toilet as a public convenience at the Great Exhibition, an international exhibition which took place in Hyde Park. Visitors would pay a small charge to use the facilities and thus was born the phrase, 'to spend a penny'. Over the following years, George persuaded local authorities to provide public conveniences across the city. These were often underground to take up as little space as possible and to try and keep offensive smells off the streets.

Lots of these public conveniences unfortunately were closed after World War Two and never reopened. Some are still locked up and unused, but others have been converted into swanky underground clubs and cocktail bars. Perhaps they serve a 'Pee-na Colada' or a 'Pong Island Iced Tea'…

Taking the Pissoir

What: Victorian urinals
Where: Star Yard, WC2A 2JL

On a little side street called Star Yard in Holborn, you will find a brilliant, rare leftover from Victorian London.

It is an iron Victorian urinal or the far more flamboyant French term: *pissoir*, dating from 1851. They would have once been common across the city but this is, as far as I can tell, the only one left in central London.

Do not go running here today if you are in need of a *pissoir*, however, as it is currently owned by the property next to it and used, it seems, as storage.

Splashback

What: Urine deflectors
Where: Clifford's Inn Passage, EC4A 2AT; Bank of England, Lothbury, EC2R 7HH; Tower Bridge Stairs, SE1 2UP

A popular addition to the outside of buildings in the 19th century, particularly down narrow alleyways or dark corners, was the urine deflector. They are essentially sloped overhangs by a wall or corner to deter people from urinating there. Anyone attempting to relieve themselves would have their urine deflected back onto their shoes.

Causing a Stink

What: *Victorian stink pipes*
Where: *77 Union Street, SE1 1SG; Chelsea Embankment, SW3 4LW; Jamaica Road, SE1 2YU; Palmerston Road, Carshalton, SM5 2JZ*

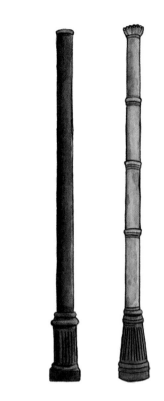

In the 1860s–70s, London was given a brand-new sewage system designed by Sir Joseph Bazalgette. The system officially opened in 1865 but was fully completed in 1875.

One immediate problem, however, was how to ventilate the sewers and release the malodorous and potentially explosive gases. The flamboyantly named Sir Goldsworthy Gurney, came up with the less flamboyantly named 'stink pipe': a cast-iron, hollow pole with an opening at the top to release the gases.

At street level they look a lot like lampposts, but there are a couple of identifying clues to look for. For starters they do not have a lamp at the top and are usually wider and taller than lampposts, but not always, and often display the iron manufacturer's name on the side. They are usually plain in design, painted green or grey, but are sometimes rather ornate.

Great examples can be seen on Union Street, on the Chelsea Embankment and on Jamaica Road. The most ornate I have seen is on Palmerston Road in Carshalton, way outside the centre of London, out in Sutton.

The Fart Lamp

What: *The sewer gas destructor lamp*
Where: *Carting Lane, WC2R 0DW*

On Carting Lane you will find a gas lamp that also serves a rather different purpose.

It is a 'sewer gas destructor lamp', patented by Joseph Webb in the 1890s, to extract potentially explosive methane from the sewers below. There is a dome in the roof of the sewer that collects the gas, the flame of the gas lamp (running off the ordinary gas supply) then draws up the methane through a hollow lamppost and burns it off.

As plumbing practices changed to disperse methane within individual houses' plumbing systems, the sewer gas destructor lamps were gradually replaced and this is the only remaining survivor.

It is affectionately referred to as the 'Fart Lamp' and Carting Lane has naturally gained the nickname 'Farting Lane'.

Shedding Light on the Situation

What: Gas lamps
Where: Goodwin's Court, WC2N 4BN; Dean's Yard, SW1P 3PA; Birdcage Walk, SW1H 9JJ

Gas lamps are a key part of London's heritage and cast a wonderful 'Dickensian' glow that is so evocative of the Victorian city. A great example of this can be found on the secluded Goodwin's Court near Covent Garden; you truly feel like you have stepped back in time.

The first gas lamp was created by Londoner William Murdoch in 1792 in his own home and the first well-recorded street in London to be lit with gas lamps was Pall Mall in 1807. Gas from burning coal was transported through pipes to the lamps, which would have initially been extinguished and relit every evening and morning by a team of lamplighters.

Gas lamps were installed right up until the mid-20th century but had started to decline in the late 19th century with the introduction of electricity.

There are around 1,500 left in London with the oldest one thought to be located in Dean's Yard by Westminster Abbey at over 200 years old. You can also find more old lamps, inscribed with the insignia of King George IV, on Birdcage Walk by St James's Park.

A Cover-up Job

What: *Coal-hole covers*
Where: *Gower Street, WC1E 6HJ*

If you have lived in London for any period of time, you will have no doubt walked on or over thousands of these without paying them any attention: the humble coal-hole cover.

These iron discs, usually around 30–36 centimetres (12–14 inches) in diameter can often be found outside Georgian and Victorian homes and were installed to cover the entrance of a coal chute down to a vaulted cellar underneath each house. This allowed the coalman to deliver coal to houses directly from the street.

They are sometimes rather decorative, with each ironworks producing a different design. Some will proudly display its state-of-the-art features, such as that it is 'self-locking'.

Coal-hole covers were, in some cases, used right up until the 1960s when the move away from coal, particularly after the Clean Air Act of 1956, led to many being covered over or removed. Thousands still remain, however, as a brilliant reminder of London's coal-powered past.

Coal-hole covers are everywhere, but the best places to look for them are on well-preserved Georgian or Victorian streets, such as Gower Street in Bloomsbury.

Stretching Resources

What: *World War Two stretcher fences*
Where: *Tabard Garden Estate, SE1 4XY;*
Rockingham Estate, SE1 6QQ

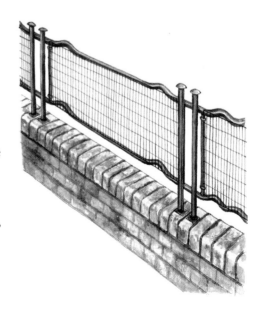

During World War Two, many of the fences around London's housing estates were salvaged for their metal to use in the war effort. After the war had finished, many were then replaced with, now superfluous, medical stretchers. Talk about recycling.

Around 600,000 stretchers had been mass produced in the run-up to the war when the government was anticipating very high civilian casualties. They, thankfully, did not need anywhere near as many.

Spot the characteristic mesh, on which the patient would lie, and the 'kink' in the metal bars, which would have been used to keep the stretcher elevated off the floor.

Pumps of Death

What: *Water pumps*
Where: *30 Cornhill, EC3V 3NF; 65–68 Leadenhall Street, EC3A 2AD; 44 Broadwick Street, W1F 7AE*

Before a widespread plumbing system to provide clean water was introduced, wells and then, later, water pumps were often a key way for Londoners to access water, particularly the poorest.

Look out for old, now defunct water pumps, mostly dating from the early-mid 19th century. You can find one on Cornhill in the City, on Queen's Square in Holborn and at the corner of Fenchurch Street and Leadenhall Street.

The one on Leadenhall Street is known as the Aldgate Pump, or the 'Pump of Death', as it is notorious for having caused the deaths of hundreds of unsuspecting Londoners from the 1860s onwards. The water supply had been running through a series of nearby graveyards and 'organic matter' was seeping into the pipes. Hundreds started dying in the 'Aldgate Pump epidemic'. The supply was eventually changed and the pump's position altered slightly in 1876, thankfully solving the problem.

On Broadwick Street in Soho, you'll find the John Snow pump. No, nothing to do with a certain *Game of Thrones* character; it was this pump that the scientist John Snow studied to work out that the cholera epidemics plaguing Victorian London were spread by unclean water.

The Fountain That Has Seen It All

What: *Water fountains*
Where: *Holy Sepulchre, EC1A 2DQ*

Between the 1830s and 1860s, London saw a series of horrific cholera outbreaks. Physician John Snow identified that this deadly epidemic was being spread partly by the contaminated water of certain pumps in the city.

In 1859, MP and philanthropist Samuel Gurney and barrister Edward Wakefield set up the Metropolitan Free Drinking Fountain Association to provide free, clean, safe drinking water to Londoners.

There was strong support from the church and temperance movement, meaning that fountains were often put next to churches. The first water fountain, set up in 1859, still survives to this day, set into the railings of Holy Sepulchre church on Holborn Viaduct, complete with its copper drinking cups.

It was incredibly popular, with an estimated 7,000 people using it every day. Up until 1868, public executions took place across the road at Newgate Prison, often with huge crowds turning up to watch. An execution was considered a great day out in 19th-century London and this fountain would therefore no doubt have been used by thousands of thirsty spectators.

The society went on to build 85 fountains in London over the following six years, many of which still survive.

Moo-ving with the Times

What: *Cattle troughs*
Where: *London Wall, EC2Y 5BL; Hopton Street, SE1 9JJ; Albany Street, NW1 4HR*

In 1867 the Metropolitan Free Drinking Water Association, providing clean, free water to Londoners via drinking fountains, teamed up with the RSPCA to also provide troughs for horses, dogs and cattle in the city. They became the snappily named

Metropolitan Drinking Fountain and Cattle Trough Association.

By 1879 there were 575 fountains and 597 troughs across the city. The troughs were produced right up until 1936 when they were phased out due to the rise of the motor car.

Many were initially made of iron or zinc-lined timber, but it is the later granite ones that survive to this day. They are now sometimes used as flower beds and can be identified by the name of the association on the side. Examples can be found on London Wall, Hopton Street and Albany Street.

Camels by the Thames

What: Camel benches
Where: Victoria Embankment, EC4Y 0HJ;
Albert Embankment, SE1 7LB

In the 1860s and 1870s, civil engineer Joseph Bazalgette masterminded a new sewage system for London that would take the sewage away from the city. To run major new sewers, still in use today, he reclaimed roughly 90,000 square metres (22 acres) worth of land from

the river and built the Victoria, Albert and, later, Chelsea embankments.

Naturally the new riverside promenades needed a bit of decoration and design submissions were taken for the street furniture. In true Victorian style, they were brilliantly elaborate.

Sit on a bench on one of the embankments and you may well be resting your arm on the head of a sphinx or swan. You will even find camel-style benches towards Blackfriars Bridge on the Victoria Embankment.

They were designed by George Vulliamy, superintending architect of the Metropolitan Board of Works, to complement the ancient Egyptian

Cleopatra's Needle (see p.97 for more on this). He also designed the two huge sphinxes flanking the Needle.

A Bit Fishy

What: Dolphin lampposts
Where: The Thames embankments

All along the Thames embankments you will see dolphin lampposts adorning the walkways.

Despite the name, these cast-iron lampposts do not actually depict dolphins but two sturgeons with the face of Neptune, the Roman god of the sea, in the centre. Many of the originals from 1870 still exist and lots have been added as the embankments have been further developed.

The lampposts were designed by George Vulliamy, the super-intending architect of the Metropolitan Board of Works.

Geoffrey Barkington of Houndsditch

What: A paw-fect bench in the City
Where: Jubilee Gardens, Houndsditch, EC2M 4WD

In 2018 the London Festival of Architecture introduced nine new unique benches to the Square Mile and the area around London Bridge, created by various designers.

My personal favourite: a stone bench on Houndsditch, with the cut-out of a long sausage dog in the middle.

It was designed by Patrick McEvoy and is a play on the name of the road but also commemorates Geoffrey Barkington, his deceased sausage dog. A plaque reads: 'Here lies Geoffrey Barkington of Houndsditch... aged 98 in dog years. May he rest in peace.'

A Whole Lot of Hot Air

What: Sneaky air vents
Where: Paternoster Square, EC1A 7BA; Soho Square, W1D 3QP; Cornhill, EC3V 3NR

Hidden beneath the bustling city is a whole other world of tunnels, basements, Tube lines and bunkers. What does this underground metropolis require? Vents! You will find air vents all over the city if you know where to look. Some have been cleverly disguised and some have been decorated to create something really rather beautiful. Here are three of my favourites.

The Paternoster Square Column, built in 2003, commemorates the two Great Fires of London in 1666 and 1940, during the Blitz. It also doubles up as a ventilation shaft for a car park beneath. Spot the tell-tale vents in the base.

The neo-Tudor style hut in the centre of Soho Square, built in 1925, was constructed to disguise a vent for an electrical substation below. It also doubles up as a maintenance cupboard.

Outside the Royal Exchange, you will find a statue of James Henry Greathead. The plinth doubles as a ventilation shaft for Bank Underground station. Fittingly, Greathead was the engineer who pioneered the method of digging deep-level tunnels for the London Underground.

A Cabbie's Comfort

What: Green cabbies' shelters
Where: Temple Place, WC2R 2PH; Embankment Place, WC2N 5AQ; Russell Square, WC1H 0XG

On London's streets, look out for rectangular green huts by the side of the road. These are Victorian cabmen's shelters, operated by the Cabmen's Shelter Fund, established in 1875.

One cold and snowy night towards the end of the 19th century, a newspaper editor named George Armstrong tried to hail a hackney carriage but there were no drivers to be seen. They were all found sheltering (and drinking) in the nearby pub. At this time drivers and their horses

were exposed to the elements while waiting for customers, so would often leave their carriages in particularly inclement weather.

Armstrong enlisted the help of the Earl of Shaftesbury and other philanthropists to set up a trust to ensure that cabbies had a place to sit, have a hot meal and, most importantly, not drink alcohol before careering around the streets of London.

From 1875–1914, 61 shelters were constructed, all the same width as a carriage, so that they could be placed on the side of public highways. They had a small kitchen and could fit up to 13 men seated inside.

After World War One, many were demolished when streets were widened or lost to bombing and there are just 13 left in London today. A few are sadly currently unused and a bit worse for wear; others you will be able to buy a cup of tea or bacon sandwich from, but the inside is still strictly reserved for cabbies.

An Oddity on Bankside

What: The Ferryman's Seat
Where: Bankside, SE1 9DS

Sat generally unnoticed by the passing masses on Bankside is a brilliant little relic: the Ferryman's Seat.

Before 1750 there was just one bridge across the Thames in central London: London Bridge. The business of ferrying people across and along the river in small

ferries was therefore a thriving one. The south bank of the river, being outside the control of the City of London, particularly in the 16th and 17th centuries, was a top destination for those seeking all sorts of 'leisure' venues such as theatres, bear-baiting pits and brothels.

The Ferryman's Seat would have been one of probably many perches by the river for the ferrymen to sit on while waiting for customers to emerge following their merriment.

Nobody knows when the seat dates from, but it is thought to potentially be hundreds of years old.

The Rest Is History

What: The Piccadilly porters' rest
Where: Piccadilly, W1J 7NW

Sitting next to a bus stop on Piccadilly is a piece of street furniture you will see nowhere else in London: the humble porters' rest.

Thousands of porters were employed in the city from the 17th–19th centuries, to transport goods around London. Porters' rests could be commonly found outside inns or on major thoroughfares in and out of the city, such as Piccadilly, for porters to lean on or to rest their baggage while they caught their breath. Being at around chest height, using them meant goods did not have to be picked up from the floor to continue the journey. The porter

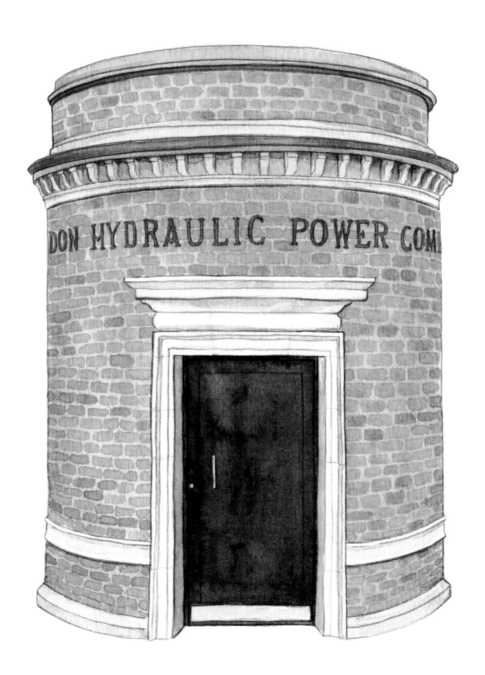

trade declined in the second half of the 19th century after the widespread introduction of the penny post and the arrival of railways that often employed their own teams. The porters' rests gradually disappeared, along with the trade. That is, all bar one.

It stood on Piccadilly, a relic of its time, until around 2014 when sadly it mysteriously disappeared. No one knows what happened to it, but following a spirited campaign, spearheaded by a local tour guide, Westminster council replaced it with a replica in 2016. It's a great shame that it's not the original, but brilliant that they replaced it as a reminder of London's past.

This spot marked the northern entrance to the Tower Subway. Opened in 1870, it was the second foot tunnel running under the Thames, after the Wapping to Rotherhithe tunnel. At first, passengers would be pulled through the tunnel in carts by cables, but this was scrapped after a year and it became a pedestrian tunnel. It closed in 1897 after Tower Bridge opened and somewhat took away its raison d'être.

The tunnel was then purchased by London Hydraulic Power Company to store its hydraulic tubes. It still holds cables and pipes today, with the current entrance being a 1920s replacement.

The Secret Tunnel by the Tower of London

What: *The Tower Subway entrance*
Where: *Petty Wales, EC3R 5BT*

Near the entrance to the Tower of London you can spot a mysterious cylindrical, brick building that looks a bit like it could be a public toilet. The clue to its real purpose is around the top where it says 'Tower Subway constructed AD 1868 London Hydraulic Power Company'.

Step to It

What: *The Duke of Wellington's mounting block*
Where: *The Athenaeum Club, Pall Mall, SW1Y 5ER*

Built 1827–30, the Athenaeum Club in St James's is a gloriously cream-hued, neo-classical building. It was designed by the eminent Regency architect Decimus Burton and is a real feast for the eyes with its decorative frieze and sculptures.

Turn away from that, however, and look at the pavement outside. You will see a long granite

block with a shorter one on top. They form a mounting block for getting on and off a horse. It was placed there at the request of one of the club's members, none other than the Iron Duke himself, the Duke of Wellington. He was Prime Minister from 1828–1830 and again in 1834 and, being in his 60s and travelling to the club on horseback, he wanted to be able to mount and dismount with grace and ease.

The Mystery of the London Stone

What: *The London Stone*
Where: *111 Cannon Street, EC4N 5AR*

One of the most mysterious objects on the streets of the capital is the London Stone.

Firstly, what is it? It is a block of oolitic limestone, of undetermined age, although some say it could date back to Roman times. It once stood at the end of Candlewick Street (now Cannon Street), opposite St Swithin's Church. Its location was first recorded here in the 12th century and in 1557 the church was known as St Swithin's at London Stone.

It has been an important London landmark for centuries, possibly millennia, and there are various theories as to its original usage.

Some think it could be a Roman milliarium or milestone, from which to measure distances. (Hence why I have put it in this chapter!) Interestingly, it stood right at the centre of a new street layout created by King Alfred the Great after AD 886, so potentially had some sort of significance for the Saxons.

In 1450 Jack Cade, leader of the Kentish rebellion against King Henry VI, struck the stone with his sword and declared himself 'lord of this city'. These events appear in Shakespeare's *Henry VI Part 2*, but the action of striking the stone has no other known recordings, so the potential significance has been lost.

One of the most persistent myths about the stone is that if it is destroyed, London will fall. Until recently it was kept behind a metal grille but has now been given a nice new secure casing at 111 Cannon Street. So, go and see the stone for yourself but, for goodness' sake, don't destroy it.

A Grave Situation

What: *Sir John Soane's tomb*
Where: *St Pancras Gardens, NW1 1UL*

In St Pancras Gardens, you will find a tomb that looks similar in shape to the traditional red telephone box. Or rather, I should say, all around London you will see red telephone boxes in the shape of a tomb.

Sir John Soane was a neo-classical architect, best known for designing the Bank of England and his amazingly extravagant house, now Sir John Soane's Museum, in Lincoln's Inn Fields.

When his wife died in 1815, he designed a tomb in which he was also buried when he died in 1837. The square-sided tomb has a domed top over segmental curves and is said to have, at least partly, inspired the design of Sir Giles Gilbert Scott's iconic K2 red telephone box in the 1920s (see p.136). Scott was, for a time, a trustee at Sir John Soane's Museum.

The Creation of an Icon

What: *The original prototype K2 red telephone box*
Where: *Burlington House, W1J 0BD*

One of Britain's most iconic symbols is, of course, the red telephone box.

There are two types of traditional red telephone box to look out for in London: the K2 and the K6. The K2 was introduced in 1926, designed by Sir Giles Gilbert Scott and selected after a post-office-sponsored competition. The K2 is larger with smaller, evenly sized, rectangular windows and the crown symbol at the top has ventilation holes in it.

In 1935 a lighter and smaller version, the K6, was designed by Scott, with larger, horizontally arranged windows and no ventilation holes in the crown.

Go to Burlington House on Piccadilly, home to the Royal Academy, and you will find, tucked into the arched entranceway, the original wooden prototype for the K2 telephone box.

The Law of the Landline

What: Blue police telephone points
Where: St Martin's Le Grand, EC1A 4AS;
Piccadilly Circus, W1B 5DQ; 232 Earl's Court
Road, SW5 9RD

Before mobile phones and the widespread use of radios, citizens and policemen on the beat needed a quick way to report a crime or ask for back up. From the late 1920s until the 1960s, blue police telephone points were located all over the city for this purpose. A beacon on top would alert any nearby policemen that trouble was a-foot.

They were phased out from the 1960s with the introduction of personal radios and there are very few left.

In 1929 the larger blue police telephone box was introduced, most famous today for being the exterior of Doctor Who's TARDIS. Outside Earl's Court station, you will find a modern version of one of these, built in 1996.

IN A 2015 NATIONAL POLL,
THE RED TELEPHONE BOX
WAS NAMED THE GREATEST
BRITISH DESIGN OF ALL TIME,
AHEAD OF THE ROUTEMASTER
DOUBLE DECKER BUS IN
SECOND PLACE AND THE
UNION JACK IN THIRD.

I'm Hooked

What: The Metropolitan Police hook
Where: 4 Great Newport Street, WC2H 7JB

At a busy intersection near Leicester Square, there is a tiny, easy-to-miss urban curiosity. It is a small metal hook with 'Metropolitan Police' written above it. The story goes that in the 1930s and 1940s a policeman was stationed at this busy road junction to direct traffic. On hot days the police would hang their heavy coats on a convenient nail sticking out of the wall at 4 Great Newport Street while construction work was going on.

Upon completion of the building work, the nail was removed, leaving the police without their handy hook! They then apparently politely requested that the building's owners install a new hook for them, to which they kindly acquiesced.

The historical evidence is unfortunately very limited to verify the story, but it seems as good an origin story as any.

London's Smallest Police Station

What: Trafalgar Square police look-out post
Where: Trafalgar Square, WC2N 5DP

In the south-east corner of Trafalgar Square you will find what is often referred to as London's smallest police station.

It was built in the 1920s to keep an eye on the, at times, volatile Trafalgar Square. It had a phone linked to Scotland Yard and a beacon on top for alerting nearby police officers. It is not really a police station, more of a look-out post, but still a fantastic oddity missed by thousands every day.

Today it is used as a maintenance and storage cupboard.

Here Be Dragons

What: City of London dragon sculptures
Where: Temple Bar Column, EC4A 2LT;
Victoria Embankment, WC2R 2PN

As you cross into the City of London along a major thoroughfare, you will no doubt pass by one of the 13 dragon statues that mark the edge of the jurisdiction of the City.

The dragon has been on the crest of the City of London, 'supporting' the shield, since the 17th century and when the Temple Bar gateway on Fleet Street was removed in 1878 to ease congestion, the Temple Bar column was designed with a large fearsome bronze dragon statue atop it, designed by Charles Bell Birch in 1880. This pretty much marks the point where the City of London becomes the City of Westminster.

Two dragon statues were then salvaged when the Coal Exchange, built in 1849, was demolished in 1962, and these were placed on the Victoria Embankment. These more petite sculptures were used as models for more around the City, such as at the southern end of London Bridge, Aldgate High Street and High Holborn. They are painted silver with red details, such as the tongue and wings.

It's a Sign

London's Oldest Blue Plaque

What: *Blue plaques*
Where: *1 King Street, SW1Y 6QG*

Walk around London for any reasonable length of time and you will undoubtedly see a blue plaque affixed to the side of a building, usually indicating that a person worth commemorating once lived or worked there.

A plaque scheme was first proposed to Parliament in 1863 and in 1866 was taken on by the Royal Society of Arts, making it the oldest scheme of its kind in the world. The Royal Society of Arts ran the scheme for 35 years, in which time they put up 35 plaques, half of which survive. The oldest surviving plaque is for Napoleon III, erected in 1867 at 1 King Street in Westminster where he lived in 1848. He was Napoleon I's nephew and was exiled to Britain after the Battle of Waterloo.

The original plaques were made by Minton, Hollins & Co pottery factory and were initially in a variety of colours, with most actually being brown.

In 1901 the London County Council took over the scheme and experimented with the design, with most up to World War Two having a laurel wreath emblem around the outside. Blue ceramic plaques became the standard from 1921 and the simple modern design of the blue plaque we see most commonly today was born in 1938.

English Heritage took over the scheme in 1986 and there are now over 900 commemorative plaques in London. Other bodies, such as specific boroughs, run their own plaques schemes as well.

London's Quirkiest Blue Plaque?

What: *Blue plaques to unusual characters*
Where: *36 Panton Street, SW1Y 4EA; 7 Bruce Grove, N17 6RA; 60 Thornhill Square, N1 1BE*

There are lots of weird and wonderful 'blue' plaques in London. Here are three of my favourites.

Tom Cribb: 'Bare Knuckle Fighter', found at the Tom Cribb pub on Panton Street just off Leicester Square. Tom Cribb was Britain's bare-knuckle fighting champion from 1809 to 1822 and the publican at the pub here in the 1820s and 1830s.

Luke Howard: 'Namer of Clouds', found on Bruce Grove. In a paper published in 1803 to the philosophical Askesian Society, of which he was a founder, Howard proposed the cloud-naming system based on characteristics such as height and substance, still in use today including cumulus, cirrus and nimbus.

Edith Garrud: 'The suffragette that knew jiu-jitsu'. Edith was a key member of the suffragette movement and in the run up to World War One trained as a jiu-jitsu instructor. She trained a core group of suffragettes in the martial art, who then formed a defensive group called 'The Bodyguard' for the increasingly volatile suffragette protests and marches. Her plaque is actually a green Islington People's Plaque and can be found at 60 Thornhill Square.

Warning Sign

What: *'Commit no nuisance' sign*
Where: *Doyce Street, SE1 0EU*

As you walk around London, if you plan on being a nuisance, you may well be put off from doing so by a 'Commit No Nuisance' sign.

These signs were put up in the late Victorian and Edwardian periods to deter people from a particular type of nuisance: public urination. The 1892 London County Council General Powers Act states 'Committing Nuisance – No person shall commit any nuisance on any bridge or against the wall.' The 'against' bit is the clue to what it is referring to.

A Sorry Sight

What: *University of London's apology plaque*
Where: *Thornhaugh Street, Russell Square,*
WC1H 0XG

On Thornhaugh Street in the western corner
of Russell Square, you will find a grey stone
plaque that reads: 'The University of London
hereby records its sincere apologies that the
plans for this building were settled without
due consultation with the Russell family and
their trustees and therefore without their
approval of its design.'

In the 1950s the university purchased
some land from the Russell family, aka the
Dukes of Bedford, on the north-west corner
of Russell Square for the construction the
Brunei Gallery.

The building was finished in 1997 but
without sign-off from the Russell family
for the design, which had been part of the
original agreement. This rather penitent
plaque was therefore put up by way of
an apology. It's unclear whether it was
demanded by the family or was a gesture
of goodwill from the university.

THE RUSSELL FAMILY ARE
THE LARGEST PRIVATE
LANDOWNERS IN BLOOMSBURY
WITH OVER 200 PROPERTIES:
A LAND HOLDING DATING
BACK TO 1669.

Ghost Signs

What: *Old shop or advertisement signs*
Where: *42 Brushfield Street, E1 6AG*

Sometimes faded and indistinct and
sometimes well-preserved or restored,
London's ghost signs are fantastic spectral
windows into the past.

They are usually old signs for shops
or product advertisements. Spitalfields,
in particular, has a great array of ghost
shop signs. This is due in large part to the
admirable efforts of locals, such as designer
Jim Howett, who have restored many.

At 42 Brushfield Street you will find
a ghost shop sign that reads: 'A. Gold.
French Milliner.'

From 1881 to 1914 over 2.5 million
Jews left Eastern Europe, fleeing religious
persecution. Lots went to America but
many also came to London. From 1880
to 1970, Spitalfields had a predominantly
Jewish population and, in fact, was one of
the largest Jewish communities in Europe.

Annie Gold and her husband Jacob
were two of these Jewish migrants. She
set up her French millinery (hat-making)
business here at 42 Brushfield Street in 1889
and lived above the shop with her husband
Jacob until 1892.

Hanging Around

What: Hanging signs
Where: Lombard Street, EC3V 9LJ

Door numbers were slowly introduced to London from the early 1700s onwards, but before being widespread, businesses would often compete with bigger and more prominent hanging signs outside their establishment, projecting into the street, to use as a location identifier and to catch the attention of passing customers.

This turned into a bit of a hazard. The story goes that Frying Pan Alley in Spitalfields got its name from an ironmonger shop that once stood on the street with a large cast-iron frying pan hanging outside as its sign. It dropped off one day, flattening a passer-by. From then on, shoppers in the know would walk on the other side of the road and 'Frying Pan Alley' stuck as its name.

In the late 1700s, hanging signs outside shops were banned, but walk down Lombard Street in the City of London and

BOTH THE BLUE EAGLE OF BARCLAYS AND THE BLACK HORSE OF LLOYDS BANK COME FROM SIGNS ONCE HANGING OUTSIDE THEIR PREMISES ON LOMBARD STREET. THE SIGNS WERE BOTH ORIGINALLY RELATED TO PREVIOUS ESTABLISHMENTS ON THE SITE.

be transported back in time. Thirty-two replica hanging signs were re-erected here to celebrate King Edward VII's coronation in 1902, four of which remain.

Look out for the cat and fiddle relating to a second-hand clothes shop located here in the medieval period and the grasshopper, the personal symbol of Thomas Gresham, a Tudor financier, who founded the nearby Royal Exchange in 1571.

Take Courage

What: Courage Brewery ghost sign
Where: 2 Redcross Way, SE1 9HR

Weary commuters gazing wistfully out of the window on the train out of London Bridge will aptly be presented with a sign telling them to 'Take Courage'.

Painted after 1955 by Courage Brewery, the 'Take Courage' sign is one of London's most iconic ghost signs.

Courage Brewery was founded in 1787 in Bermondsey and merged with Barclay Perkins & Co in 1955. The building with the ghost sign was once part of the Anchor Brewery, which at the beginning of the 19th century was not just the largest brewery in London in terms of output but the entire world.

Walk III

Heading South of the river to hunt down some of London's quirkiest street furniture.

1 Southwark Cathedral (see Going Gothic, p.18)

2 Winchester Palace ruins (see The Ruins of a Medieval Palace, p.17)

3 Bankside cannon bollard (see Bollard Battles, p.109)

4 The Ferryman's Seat (see An Oddity on Bankside, p.131)

5 Bear Gardens (see Freedom to Bear Arms, p.63)

6 Courage Brewery ghost sign (see Take Courage, p.145)

7 The Wheatsheaf (see A Cheeky Half, p.45)

8 The George Inn (see London's Last Galleried Coaching Inn, p.26)

9 The King's Arms (see London Bridge Is Falling Down, p.20)

10 Victorian stink pipe (see Causing a Stink, p.122)

11 'Commit no nuisance' sign (see Warning Sign, p.141)

12 Lord Clyde (see Temples of Intemperance, p.41)

13 Tabard Gardens war stretcher railings (see Stretching Resources, p.124)

14 Alfred the Great statue (see Where Is the Oldest Statue in London?, p.98)

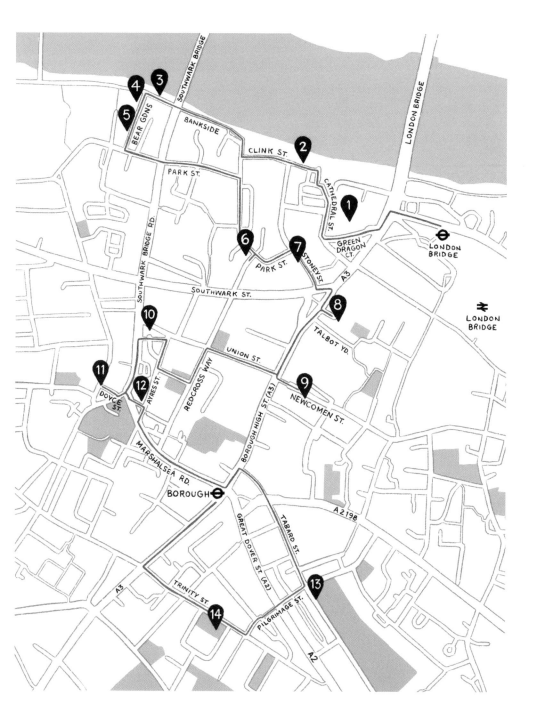

IV. IT'S ONLY NATURAL

Beneath the urban sprawl of London — the streets, skyscrapers and modernity — lies London's natural terrain: the rocks, the hills and the rivers. As well as showing you where to see the clues to this now often hidden landscape, this chapter will also look at London's plethora of green spaces, from the sweeping royal parks to the tiny, secret pocket gardens.

London's Rivers: Lost and Found

EVIDENCE OF LONDON'S LOST RIVERS AND SECRET SPOTS ALONG THE THAMES

A Secret London Beach

What: *The London foreshore*
Where: *Prospect of Whitby, E1W 3SH*

If there is one thing you can rely on in London it is that the Thames will rise and fall twice a day.

Missed by many as they go about their daily business, at low tide, look down at the foreshore and you may well begin to notice a whole other world. You will often see a diverse mix of birdlife, such as seagulls, herons and cormorants. Or you may spot waterproof-clad humans, walking slowly, eyes focused to the ground. These are 'mudlarks'. In the 18th and 19th centuries, mudlarks were the poorest in society, trying to scratch a living from the bits of rope, coal or anything else they could find on the banks of the river. Today mudlarks are enthusiasts who scour the foreshore for any historical treasures offered up by the last tide.

You need a licence to mudlark and some stretches of the foreshore are out of bounds. There are sections, however, that the general public can access, such as the 'secret beach' behind the Prospect of Whitby pub in Wapping. Do not be alarmed by the replica gallows here: this is a nod to 'Execution Dock', which once stood near this spot, where pirates would be hanged.

FOR ONE OF THE BEST
VIEWS OF TOWER BRIDGE,
HEAD TO HORSLEYDOWN
STAIRS, JUST OFF SHAD
THAMES, TO FIND A SMALL
SECTION OF FORESHORE,
RIGHT NEXT TO THE BRIDGE.

'When the lions drink, London will sink. When it's up to their manes, we'll go down the drains', i.e., if the tide reaches as high as the lion heads, London will flood. This however does not apply anymore. Twelve inches were added in the years before the construction of the Thames Barrier as tides got higher.

'When the Lions Drink, London Will Sink'

What: *A tide-monitoring station and lion-head mooring rings*
Where: *Victoria Embankment, SW1A 2JH; Albert Embankment SE1 7SP*

By the north end of Westminster Bridge, look out for what looks like a strange blue-green kiosk. There are not many clues on the outside to its true identity, but step onto the small rungs to peer inside and you will spot a computer display with a number on it. This strange kiosk is, in fact, a tide-monitoring station, measuring height above sea level.

Measures have had to be put in place to ensure that London does not flood, particularly as sea levels rise, with the Thames Barrier, constructed in 1984, being the most significant measure. On the embankments, look out for a series of lion-head mooring rings, added in 1868. An old London adage once stated that

As Old as the Hills

What: *London's hills and lost rivers*
Where: *Farringdon Road, EC1M 3LL; Ludgate Hill, EC4M 7AA; Cornhill, EC3V 3ND; Bond Street station, W1R 1FE*

The area now occupied by the ever-growing metropolis was once criss-crossed by rivers and streams feeding into the Thames.

These were pretty much all swallowed up, subsumed into the drainage system beneath the city as it grew, and often still flow in pipes beneath our feet.

Evidence of these lost waterways is all around you as you walk through London: in the street names, the shapes of roads and in the undulations of the ground.

Walk down Farringdon Road to Blackfriars Bridge, look to either side and you will notice the ground gently rising away from you; this is because you are walking along the valley of the River Fleet. Similarly, if you walk from Ludgate Hill by St Paul's Cathedral, along Cannon Street and head to Cornhill, you will have crossed the valley of the River Walbrook. Ludgate Hill and Cornhill are two hills split by this now lost river. Walk along Oxford Street and by Bond Street station you will notice a dip in the road that marks the course of the River Tyburn.

The Winding Road

What: Marylebone Lane
Where: Marylebone Lane, W1U 2NE

Walk through Marylebone and you may notice that generally the street pattern is pretty orderly, with a grid of straight roads, laid out in the 18th century as London expanded westwards. Winding its way through the grid, however, is Marylebone Lane. The reason for its exceptionalism is that this route pre-dates the other streets

and follows the course of the River Tyburn, now buried beneath the streets.

The name 'Marylebone' is thought to reference St Mary's church on the 'bourne': an old English name for a river. You also see this in 'Holborn', meaning a hollow brook or river, as the now buried River Fleet once flowed through it, and 'Kilburn' coming from the old English 'Cye-bourne', meaning royal river, references the River Westbourne.

An Ear to the Ground

What: Places to hear and see the River Fleet
Where: 26–28 Ray Street, EC1R 3DJ; Greville Street, EC1N 8SS

There are a few spots where you can actually hear, and sometimes even see, the River Fleet flowing underground on its way from Hampstead Heath to Blackfriars Bridge where it enters the Thames.

There is a drain cover outside the Coach pub on Ray Street through which you can hear and, sometimes, see the Fleet flowing. It helps if it has been raining recently. There is a similar grate at the corner of Greville Street and Saffron Hill.

Taking the Tube

What: *The River Westbourne in Sloane Square station*
Where: *Sloane Square station, SW1W 8BB; Ingestre Road, NW5 1UF*

The Thames tributaries may be buried, subsumed into the storm drain system, but at some locations, where the ground level has been lowered for train tracks or Underground stations, you can actually see the pipes through which the rivers flow. For example, at Sloane Square Tube station, look up and you will see a large green pipe suspended above your head, containing the River Westbourne.

If you go to Ingestre Road in Kentish Town and cross the railway footbridge there, look over the side and you will see a large black pipe leading over the tracks. This carries one leg of the River Fleet.

A Lost London Island

What: Thorney Island
Where: Lambeth Bridge, SW1P 3JR

The now buried River Tyburn is thought to have split into multiple legs and formed what was essentially a river delta before it met the Thames in Pimlico and Westminster. Two of these streams formed a raised area of land, surrounded by low-lying marshland, known as Thorney Island.

This was where Edward the Confessor established the Palace of Westminster and Westminster Abbey after his coronation in 1042.

If you look to the Westminster edge of the river from the northern side of Lambeth Bridge at low tide, you will see a storm relief outlet down at the foreshore. After heavy rains, one leg of the Tyburn still flows into the Thames here.

Well, Well

What: *Evidence of old wells*
Where: *14–16 Farringdon Lane, EC1R 3AU;*
61–63 King's Cross Road, WC1X 9LN;
Well Walk, NW3 1LH

London's lost rivers and Thames tributaries once played important roles in the everyday lives of Londoners. The remnants of wells that drew up waters from the springs around the rivers are an example of this.

Peer through a window at 14–16 Farringdon Lane, by the course of the River Fleet, and you will see the 'Clerks' Well', that once supplied the monastery here with water and gave 'Clerkenwell' its name. On King's Cross Road, look out for a mysterious plaque that states 'This is Bagnigge House. Neare the Pindera Wakefeilde, 1680.' Bagnigge House is thought to have been near this site since at least 1680 and became a popular spa destination after springs were discovered here in the 18th century. The 'Pinder of Wakefield' is thought to be a pub local to Bagnigge House.

On Well Walk in Hampstead, where many of the lost rivers originate, you will find the Chalybeate Well, 'Chalybeate', meaning rich in iron. It was the spring water from this well that, from at least 1700, turned the village of Hampstead into a health resort for the wealthy.

Flora and Fauna

LEAFY LANDMARKS AND HIDDEN OASES OF CALM

Regent's Park's Prehistoric Secret

What: Fossilised tree trunks
Where: Queen Mary's Rose Gardens, NW1 4NR

Hiding in plain sight at the meeting of two paths in Regent's Park is a prehistoric surprise: a group of fossilised tree trunk stumps thought to be 20–100 million years old.

Queen Mary's Gardens, where the tree trunks can be found, were established in 1932 but, prior to that, since the 1840s, the space was leased by the Royal Botanic Society. The Society grew a huge variety of specimens here, held horticultural shows and ran a museum on the site. It was in this period that the prehistoric trunks were acquired

and seem to have been left after the Society vacated the space in 1932. The stumps are thought to be from coniferous trees laid down in Lower Purbeck in Dorset.

Plane-speaking

What: *The London plane tree*
Where: *Berkeley Square, W1J 6EA;*
Victoria Embankment, SW1A 2JH

Did you know London is officially a forest? One-fifth of the capital is under tree cover, making it, by UN standards, an urban forest.

The most common species of tree seen on London's streets is the London plane tree. It is thought to be a hybrid of the American sycamore and the Oriental plane and was first cultivated here in the 17th century. The species was then widely planted across the city from the 18th century onwards and was particularly popular in smog-ridden Victorian London due to its pollution-resistant qualities. As well as regularly shedding its bark, it also does not mind having its roots compacted under concrete and tarmac, making it very suitable for urban planting.

Some of the oldest plane trees in the city can be found on Berkeley Square in Mayfair, planted in 1789. The embankments are also great spots for admiring these majestic trees.

A Royal Oak

What: *Queen Elizabeth's Oak*
Where: *Greenwich Park, SE10 9NN*

In Greenwich Park you will find the remains of a once mighty oak tree imbued with history and legend. It is known as 'Queen Elizabeth's Oak' and is thought to have been planted as far back as the 12th century. For context, that is the century when Richard the Lionheart went on Crusade and Thomas Becket was murdered.

Legend has it that King Henry VIII, who loved to hunt in Greenwich Park, once danced around this oak with his beloved Anne Boleyn. The name comes from the story that Queen Elizabeth I once picnicked in the shade of its leafy boughs.

It reputedly also had a hollow trunk that was, at one time, used as a lock-up for troublemakers in the park.

Queen Elizabeth's Oak died in the 1800s but remained standing due to the ivy encasing it, before blowing down finally in 1991 during a heavy storm. What is left today is, therefore, sadly a shadow of its former glory. Next to it you will see another oak tree planted by the Duke of Edinburgh in 1992. Who knows what that tree may see in its lifetime!

Blow Up Bridge

What: *Macclesfield Bridge*
Where: *Avenue Road, NW8 7PU*

Winding its way quietly around central London from Limehouse in the east to Paddington in the west is the Regent's Canal. Opened in 1820, it was once an industrial artery transporting goods, namely coal, by barge around the city.

Today it is a thread of nature and greenery, perfect for interesting and tranquil walks. Along the route you can see clues to its industrial past, such as the old coal office ghost sign and coal-drop buildings at King's Cross, now swanky restaurants, shops and bars. Another clue are the grooves on the handrails or columns of bridges, created by years of friction from the ropes pulled by horses to transport the barges along the canal.

These can be seen clearly on the footbridge by Camden Lock market and on the columns of Macclesfield Bridge, otherwise known as 'Blow Up Bridge'. At 3am on the 2nd October 1874, locals in the area were woken by a huge tremor. A boat carrying gunpowder up the canal had exploded just underneath Macclesfield Bridge, killing three people and destroying the bridge. When the bridge was rebuilt, the columns holding it up were put back the wrong way round, so that the grooves are on the wrong side, facing the path instead of the canal.

War and Peace

What: Pocket parks in bombed-out churches
Where: St Dunstan's Hill, EC3R 5DD;
Christchurch Greyfriars, EC1A 7BA

In some cases, the bombed-out shells of churches in the City have been retained and tranquil pocket parks established inside them. One of the most magical is St Dunstan in the East church. It was originally built around AD 1100, severely damaged in the Great Fire of London in 1666 and then restored by Sir Christopher Wren. The church was gutted by bombing in 1941 but Wren's tower and steeple survived.

In 1970 it was opened as a public garden. It is a stunning oasis in the City, particularly in autumn and spring, and is also a fantastic place to contemplate London's turbulent history of fire and resurgence. It is, of course, carefully maintained, but with ivy and climbing plants entwined around the crumbling walls and crawling through the window spaces, it gives the wonderful impression of nature slowly reclaiming the church.

Another example of a great pocket park in a bombed-out church is Christchurch Greyfriars by St Paul's Cathedral.

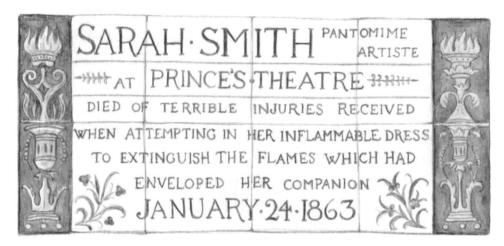

Bless You

What: *Postman's Park*
Where: *King Edward Street, EC1A 7BT*

The City of London is full of hidden green spaces and beautiful pocket parks: oases of calm amid the turbulent city.

One of the most intriguing is Postman's Park, so called because it once backed onto the General Post Office. It was formed in 1880 when three ex-churchyards were amalgamated. It is a lovely space with flower beds and trees, including a

Davidia involucrata, otherwise known as the 'handkerchief tree'. This rare tree has flowers surrounded by large white leaves that resemble handkerchiefs, particularly when fallen to the ground.

The park is also home to the Memorial to Heroic Self-Sacrifice: a wall inside a wooden shelter lined with ceramic tablets, each a memorial to someone who lost their life while saving the lives of others. Conceived by George Watts, the first four plaques were unveiled in 1900 and there are 54 in total today.

THE STREET BIRDCAGE WALK
IS SO CALLED BECAUSE
IT WOULD HAVE ONCE
BEEN WHERE KING JAMES I
KEPT HIS AVIARIES OF
EXOTIC BIRDS.

Space Invaders

What: Ring-necked parakeets
Where: Kensington Gardens, W2 3XA

Walk through one of London's parks and you may well hear some rather grating screeches overhead. The likely culprit: the ring-necked parakeet. London's parks, particularly Kensington Gardens, are home to this invasive species from West Africa and India.

No one is quite sure where exactly the first freed parakeets came from, but there are many theories, ranging from Jimi Hendrix releasing a pair in the 1960s, the Great Storm in 1987 damaging aviaries and breeding pairs escaping from the set of the film *The African Queen* at Isleworth Studios in 1951. Wherever they came from originally, they have thrived in London's parks.

If birds landing on you is your thing, then take some tempting food with you to Kensington Gardens and the parakeets will do just that.

A Feathery Gift

What: Pelicans of St James's Park
Where: St James's Park, SW1H 9AP

London is blessed with many beautiful parks and the largest proportion are made up by the Royal Parks, covering nearly 5,000 acres of land in Greater London.

The eight parks were once exclusively for the use of the royal family, predominantly as hunting grounds.

St James's Park, for example, started as a marshy area of land, which was subsequently drained and designated a royal hunting ground by King Henry VIII. King James I added a menagerie of exotic animals here in the 17th century, including crocodiles, elephants and camels. King Charles II opened the park to the public for the first time and in 1664 was given the first pelicans here as a gift by the Russian Ambassador. A colony of pelicans have been a feature in the park ever since, along with many other birds, such as tufted ducks, Egyptian geese and black swans.

The Smallest Nature Reserve in London

What: *Barnsbury Wood*
Where: *Crescent Street, N1 1BW*

Tucked away behind the grand Victorian terraces of Thornhill Crescent in Barnsbury, you will find a tiny hidden woodland. At 0.35 hectares (0.85 acres), Barnsbury Wood is London's smallest nature reserve.

The roads and houses in this area were laid out from 1813–1849 on land owned by the Thornhill family.

Barnsbury Wood was once the personal garden of George Thornhill who lived at number 7 Huntingdon Street, which was at the time the vicarage of St Andrew's Church, and many of the trees would have been planted around this time. The garden was abandoned in the early 1900s and in 1974 the Borough of Islington purchased the land for development. Thankfully plans fell through due to the awkward shape of the site and, in the end, the council decided to demolish numbers 1 and 2 Crescent Street to give public access to the space. It is managed as an ecology park and gained nature reserve status in 1996.

Wildlife found here include the common toad, the long-tailed tit and the lesser stag beetle. Despite being the smallest nature reserve in London, it is, in fact, the largest area of real woodland in Islington.

It is only open at very specific times so make sure you check the website before visiting.

Vauxhall's Secret Jungle Neighbourhood

What: *Bonnington Square*
Where: *Vauxhall, SW8 1TE*

Tucked away among the backstreets of Vauxhall, you will find Bonnington Square. Visit and you will quickly see that Bonnington Square is not just your classic square of Victorian terraced houses. It has secret garden spaces, leafy overgrown corners, vines climbing up the house fronts and both tropical and native trees planted along the pavements.

In the 1970s the Greater London Council made a compulsory purchase of the houses on Bonnington Square to demolish them and build a new school. In the interim between the residents leaving and the bulldozers arriving, squatters moved into the empty houses and, by the early 1980s, they occupied most of the square. They set up a cooperative and were able to lease and then purchase the houses from the council. They set up a wholefoods shop, a vegetarian café, community gardens and they also started the 'Paradise Project'. The idea behind the project is to bring inner-city living and nature together in harmony and fill every available space with foliage and greenery.

A Miniature Vineyard in the City

What: *Cleary Garden*
Where: *Queen Victoria Street, EC4V 2AR*

Another of the City of London's pocket parks is the lovely, terraced haven that is Cleary Garden. The site, previously occupied by houses, was left as a bombsite after the Blitz. In 1949 Joseph Brandis, a City worker and keen gardener, turned the space into a garden.

The gardens were then significantly re-landscaped in the 1980s to create what we have today. They were named after Fred Cleary, chairman of the Metropolitan Public Gardens Association, otherwise known as 'Flowering Fred' for his work in creating public gardens in the City.

In 2007 a series of grape vines were planted along the upper terraces: a gift from the winemakers of the Loire valley. This fittingly harks back to the time when this area was a hub for London's wine merchants. The best time to see the vines is in September or October when the grapes are ripening.

Walk IV

WESTMINSTER STATION TO BERKELEY SQUARE
(5.4 KM/3.4 MILES)

A green and leafy wander through royal parks and gorgeous Georgian squares.

I   Tide-monitoring station (see 'When the Lions Drink, London Will Sink', p.151)

2   Two Chairmen (see Transport Links, p.66)

3   Queen Anne's Gate (see Snuffed Out, p.31; see Getting Stoned, p.32)

4   Pelicans of St James's Park (see A Feathery Gift, p.161)

5   Admiralty Citadel (see Secret Wartime Bunker, p.50)

6   The grave of Giro (A 'Nazi' Dog Grave, see p.82)

7   The Duke of Wellington's mounting block (see Step to It, p.133)

8 King William III statue (see Mole Hills into Mountains, p.102)

9 Napoleon III blue plaque (see London's Oldest Blue Plaque, p.140)

10 Pickering Place (see London's Smallest Square, p.34)

11 The Queen's Chapel (see A Forbidden Chapel, p.28)

12 Piccadilly porters' rest (see The Rest Is History, p.131)

13 Down Street station (see Ghost Platforms, p.44)

14 Cast-iron shoe scraper at 11–13 Chesterfield Street (see Casting Around for a Solution, p.32)

15 London plane tree (see Plane-speaking, p.157)

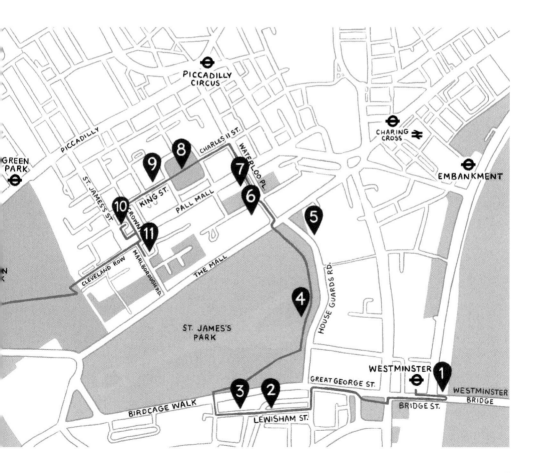

General Index

Index of Postcodes

Author Biography

Illustrator Biography

Jack Chesher is a London tour guide, blogger, historian, explorer and all-round enthusiast for the city's quirks. In 2020, Jack founded his website **Living London History** as a weekly blog, sharing London's most fascinating and unusual historical sites, as well as self-guided walks of the city.

In 2021 he completed Open City's Golden Key Academy guiding course and since October 2021 has been sharing this passion by leading public and private guided walking tours of London's hidden history. The tours are of specific areas of London, aiming to unearth its hidden history and point out the little details that you may otherwise miss as you walk around the city. The tours are very popular and in just under a year, Living London History tours shot into the top ten tours in London on Tripadvisor.

Jack grew up in Essex, a short train journey from London and has always been fascinated by the city. He studied history at the University of Bristol, where he lived for a time before moving to London properly.

To keep up with Jack, you can read his weekly blog posts and book guided tours at www.livinglondonhistory.com and can follow him @livinglondonhistory on Instagram, Facebook and TikTok and @livinglondonhis on Twitter.

Katharine Fraser is a freelance illustrator and graphic designer, born and raised in Southend-on-Sea. After studying Art & Design at UAL and the University of Brighton, she now splits her time between illustration, graphic design and photography, and has since worked on projects for Brighton University, The Courtauld Institute of Art, Clipper Lighters, and Lucy & Yak, amongst others.

Almost obsessively detail-focused and a celebrator of the underdog, most of her illustration and photography work involves capturing the overlooked, hidden gems and bringing the seemingly mundane to the forefront. She dissects the details of places and pop culture in organised illustrated prints over at Flatlay Design, and creates kitsch homeware over at Cheap Thrills, a colourful celebration of the British seaside.

When not at her desk, you can find her rifling through charity shops and vintage stores for more hidden gems, or day-tripping around the seaside towns of the UK, taking pictures and sketches of the things you may have just walked past.

Keep up with her work on the following Instagram accounts: @katharinefraser.design, @flatlaydesign and @cheapthrills.studio.

First published in 2023 by Frances Lincoln Publishing,
an imprint of The Quarto Group.
1 Triptych Place,
2nd Floor, London, SE1 9SH,
United Kingdom
T (0)20 7700 6700
www.quarto.com

A catalogue record for this book is available from the
British Library.

ISBN 978-0-7112-7755-7
Ebook ISBN 978-0-7112-7756-4

15 14

Design by Masumi Briozzo

Printed in China